WRITING FOR THE READER
Practice in Prose Craft

JEFF P. JONES

TROIKA PRESS

Published by Troika Press
Troika Press, PO Box 3331, Moscow ID 83843, U.S.A.

Writing for the Reader: Practice in Prose Craft, 2nd edition
Copyright © Jeff P. Jones, 2018, 2019
ISBN 978-1980708148

The cover image is the Troika Press logo. The horses represent Troika's dedication to quality, sustainability, and affordability.

Acknowledgments

Deepest thanks to Kim Barnes, Mary Clearman Blew, Alexander Chee, Anthony Doerr, Margot Livesey, Priscilla Long, Daniel Orozco, Joy Passanante, Scott Russell Sanders, Gary Williams, and Robert Wrigley—generous souls whose wisdom undergirds this handbook and whose extraordinary teaching belies the claim that writing cannot be taught.

Preface

This handbook offers craft practice in literary prose. Based on the commonalities of literary fiction and creative nonfiction, it embraces the principle of deliberate practice. Its aim is to get writers writing, and as such it gives only the most essential explanation of each craft technique before prompting the writer into practicing the technique itself.

For Teachers of Creative Writing

The scaffolding model in Appendix A offers a suggested sequence for the presented themes. The model also delineates introductory from intermediate themes so that students who advance levels can use the handbook in both sequences without repeating material.

CONTENTS

4

IV. ADDITIONAL EXERCISES (X1-X40)

APPENDIXES

PART I

DRAFTING

The faster you blurt, the more swiftly you write, the more honest you are. In hesitation is thought. In delay comes the effort for a style, instead of leaping upon truth which is the only style worth deadfalling or tiger-trapping.

RAY BRADBURY

FREEWRITING

We all have editors in our head constantly telling us that what we're writing is worthless, that it's stupid or naïve or cliché or just not good enough. Freewriting is a way to subvert those editors. In the same way that forcing water through a bottleneck prevents it from pooling, putting the focus on quickly generating words bypasses all those annoying voices. When you freewrite, think to yourself "Be water." Just flow and don't ever go back, don't ever erase.

Here are Natalie Goldberg's six guidelines for freewriting:
1. Keep your hand moving.
2. Don't cross out.
3. Don't worry about spelling, punctuation, grammar.
4. Lose control.
5. Don't think. Don't get logical.
6. Go for the jugular—if something comes up that's scary or naked, dive right into it.

Pure freewriting has no topic:

Example
What should i write now should i capitalize this why not does it save time why should i want to save time i'd like to eat but i'd rather keep working until i hear my stomack rumble or start to go crazy now i'm stuck i'm stuck i'm stuck with nothing to write except that my stomach yes i spelled stomach wrong earlier please stomach rumble so i can stop writing and go eat…

Doing a pure freewrite can be a good way, at the start of a writing session, to comb out all the little nagging thoughts that distract from the practice. It's a way of clearing the mind and helping it to focus.

Directed freewriting, which is usually more fruitful, takes a starting point but is completely free and open as to where it might go. Water, after all, trends along the path of least resistance, so directed freewriting really should carry that sense of freedom. Goldberg encourages writers to capture their "first thoughts"—those images or flashes of idea and sensation that occur before the second and third thoughts comment, criticize, and evaluate. We can't always capture these first thoughts, but it's worth the effort to try.

Example – directed freewrite: "Offer a bitter complaint"
Lukewarm coffee is the worst slug I've ever tried what is this shit?You mean this cafeteria really expects me to drink put this garbage in my mouth? Ugh. And the man who serves it cashiers it has the a face look of stone as if he said "thank you" or "hello" it might break his face…

Freewriting is most useful in generating prose for later revision. You should expect most of what you generate not to make the final cut. But in writing practice, nothing is wasted. Like a musician, a writer must continually practice to maintain facility in the art. You may discover, in any particular freewrite, only two words that make it into the finished piece. Consider the 98 words you end up discarding the tax on the vital 2 that are kept. If you hadn't done the freewrite, you'd never have found them.

Freewriting also relieves you of the pressure to make every sentence beautiful and lasting. It's a method for freeing your mind to be wild and associative, and it leads to creative and pleasurable connections.

Example – directed freewrite on a scene from a story
The black water ran thick in the gutter ran like oil in the gutter no like a river of black blood no it's like milk curdled and turned black and David followed its flow toward the storm drain three blocks away a foul odor of a choking odor of death and decay of rot and spoil it ran thick and fast with a heavy smoothness the angles and bends of it and ripples reflected alternately reflected then its angled ripples caught patches and reflected patches of the flat gray sky…

Practice
A. Do a pure freewrite. Time it for 3 or 4 minutes.

B. Do a 5-minute "bitter complaint" or "effusive praise" freewrite. Don't let the editors in your mind have any control over what you write. Practice simply *generating* words and don't worry about mistakes. Let the piece go where it goes.

C. Do a 10-minute freewrite on a scene from a piece you're working on. Or if you haven't started a piece yet, freewrite an opening. Just pick a topic or experience or idea and go with it.

See Additional Exercises: X1, X4, X14, X24, X25, X28, X35

Practice isn't the thing you do once you're good. It's the thing you do that makes you good.

MALCOLM GLADWELL

WRITING PRACTICE

Can writing be taught? How important is talent? Of the Beatles' apprenticeship in Hamburg before they were famous, John Lennon said, "We had to play for hours and hours on end. Every song lasted twenty minutes and had twenty solos in it. That's what improved the playing. There was nobody to copy from. We played what we liked best and the Germans liked it as long as it was loud."

The scientific and anecdotal evidence, largely from the realm of psychology, has piled up in support of deliberate practice as the most reliable means for improving one's ability in many areas, including writing. It should come as no surprise that, like any art form, writing takes practice.

Some thoughts on process
Write daily—it's the only way.
    Erik Larson

Many times I just sit for three hours with no ideas coming to me. But I know one thing: If an idea does come between 9 and 12, I am there ready for it.
    Flannery O'Connor

I hate writing but I love having written.
    Dorothy Parker

I sit down in the morning and reread the work I did the day before. And then I wool-gather, staring at the blank page or off into space. I imagine my characters, and let myself daydream about them. A movie begins to play in my head, with emotion pulsing underneath it, and I stare at it in a trancelike state, until words bounce around together and form a sentence. Then I do the menial work of getting it down on paper, because I'm the designated typist.
    Anne Lamott

But all this advice from senior writers to establish a discipline always, to get down a thousand words a day whatever one's mood, I find an absurdly puritanical and impractical approach. Writing is like eating or making love; a natural process, not an artificial one.
    John Fowles

The only secret to writing is A/C: ass in chair.
    Wayson Choy

So besieged are we by the entertainment industry, that we are being stimulated only in certain directions. The sound of fizz is everywhere. Sustained concentration on the printed word, whether in-depth argument or fictional narrative, creates a particular cerebral event which visual-dependent media cannot. The assault upon this has meant the very theft of our thinking space.
Alan Bissett

Some Tips
1. Find a routine, a dedicated time and place, that are both comfortable and without interruptions. Carve out the time to go there and write every day or every other day as a commitment to see how your writing improves over a few weeks.

2. Ease yourself into a writing schedule. Set the challenge of writing for 15 minutes each day.

3. Schedule your writing practice for the time of day when you're most energetic.

4. Keep writing if the writing's going well. If not, stop at the end of your scheduled time, congratulate yourself on meeting your commitment, and go on with your day.

Practice
A. Draft a plan for your writing practice over the next several weeks (specify the duration in your journal). Where will you write and when is best for you? How long will you write for? Commit to it.

For the past sixteen years, pretty much every single day, I've penciled a journal entry into a spiral notebook.

ANTHONY DOERR

KEEPING A JOURNAL

A journal is essential for writing practice. Think of your journal as a work-in-progress, an idea storehouse, the place you go to record the conversation you just overheard in the coffee shop, the way the light on the ash tree looked, the idea you just had for a new piece.

Practice
B. Buy a new journal. Choose it intuitively according to its physical characteristics. Do you like spiral notebooks? Fancy leather covers? Moleskines? Legal pads? Buy one that makes you want to pick it up and write in it. Put an inspirational quote on the cover.

You can't wait for inspiration. You have to go after it with a club.

JACK LONDON

INSPIRATION

How do you find inspiration? Brenda Ueland claims that she needed to walk each day for five or six miles, otherwise she suffered from depression and a lack of ideas. Others prefer to ruminate (and drink lots of coffee) until an idea strikes. Still others head for the library.

Federico Garcia Lorca describes the process of inspiration: "The imagination hunts for images using tried and true techniques of the hunt. The mechanics of poetic imagination are always the same: a concentration, a leap, a flight, a return with the treasure, and a classification and selection of what has been brought back." His description suggests the freedom the mind must have to make the initial leap into the imagination, to reach for that fresh idea, and to try to capture some of its energy.

Some thoughts
Morning is the best time; the mind after sleeping is like a white page: blank and clean.
   Alberto Moravia

If I'm ever frustrated or angry or bored, I use my body. To walk, to run, to make love, to touch.
   Natalie Diaz

I write entirely to find out what I'm thinking, what I'm looking at, what I see and what it means. What I want and what I fear.
   Joan Didion

Practice
A. Take a walk and bring your journal with you. Feel the rhythm of your steps, the pumping of your heart. Let your mind wander. Allow your thoughts to sift through all the daily detritus and settle. Wait for an interesting idea to develop. As it does, continue walking and thinking about it. Then, when you're ready, stop walking and begin to write.

B. Turn the common advice to "write what you know" on its head, and instead, write what you don't know, what puzzles and disturbs you. There's energy in what you don't understand. Embrace the unknowing. Explore your fears and desires; after all, you're the only one who can. Don't be ashamed by your subject—what counts in self-knowledge is honesty.

See Additional Exercises: X1, X3, X5, X12, X13, X24, X28, X34, X40

*When you start reading in a certain way, that's already the
beginning of your writing.*

TESS GALLAGHER

CREATIVE READING

In his essay "The American Scholar," Ralph Waldo Emerson says that "there is
creative reading as well as creative writing." He says that if the writer is
engaged in her own work, then whatever she reads will be made meaningful by
potential connections.

Emerson doesn't stop there, though. Even more provocatively, he says, "Books
are the best of things, well used; abused among the worst. What is the right use?
What is the one end, which all means go to effect? They are for nothing but to
inspire. I had better never see a book, than to be warped by its attraction clean
out of my own orbit and made a satellite instead of a system."

Be selfish in your reading. Don't read merely to admire, but make whatever
you're reading serve your own writing project. An engaged imagination will
light the world with its fire.

Some thoughts
Plant slips of paper in books so you can record ideas that occur to you while
you're reading; keep scissors and self-stick pads near newspapers and
magazines; put note cards in the kitchen, the living room, the bathroom. Then
every week or so, gather up your ideas and record them in your journal or file
them for future use.
    Rebecca McClanahan

Why were we given something as amazing as imagination if we're not going to
use it?
    Jim Shepard

Practice
A. List five things you find fascinating. Choose the one that feels most
   "radioactive" and freewrite about it. How would you approach it in prose
   and make it all your own?

B. Freewrite about a book you're currently reading or have recently read. What
   are its connections with what you're writing?

See Additional Exercises: X3, X11, X13, X21, X36; Projects J, N, O

Good writers borrow; great writers steal.

T. S. Eliot

IMITATION

We all need some goad, some kernel to get started, and imitation is a tried-and-true method for getting a new narrative off the ground.

When using imitation, think structurally. Dissect a work that you admire and note its major structural components. What type of opening does it use (see "Openings")? When do we meet the main character? How many paragraphs are spent establishing the setting? When does scene shift to summary and vice versa? When is conflict introduced? When does it intensify? Sketch the work's skeleton, then, using your own content, imitate that structure until your piece takes on its own life.

Keep in mind that we're not limited only to imitating prose artifacts. Nature, visual art, mathematics, music—all provide structures that can be imitated. Jerome Stern says, "A shape invites you to fill it," and it's useful to see shapes as taking-off points. Think about your narrative's content; what forms naturally fit it?

<u>Some thoughts</u>
Original works do not require an original structure.
> Priscilla Long

Writing is learned by imitation.
> William Zinsser

<u>Practice</u>
A. In *Bird By Bird*, Anne Lamott relates the use of a story alphabet, ABDCE, to outline a narrative. The letters stand for Action, Background, Development, Climax, and Ending. Outline a new story or essay using Lamott's story alphabet.
  A - begin with **A**ction, an *in media res* opening (see "Openings")
  B - give some **B**ackground on the characters and situation
  D - **D**evelop the characters' fears and desires, as well as the plot
  C - culminate the action in a **C**risis
  E - the **E**nding shows how the characters are significantly changed

B. Look closely at one of your favorite books. What's a technique in it that you find compelling? (e.g., character appearance, dialogue, tension, imagery, etc.). Study the use of that technique, then imitate it in a piece of your own. Append a paragraph analyzing how well your imitation came off.

See Additional Exercises: X11, X13, X21, X30, X36; Projects F, N, O

Life is our dictionary.

RALPH WALDO EMERSON

OBSERVATION

"Writers, when they write, need to approach things for the first time each time," says Natalie Goldberg. Think about your living room. Although you've probably walked into it a thousand times, try to recall the first time you entered it. Was it spacious or cramped? Did it have any particular smells? Odd colors? Sounds? Returning to the first experience of something puts the writer in the shoes of the reader to whom each encounter is fresh.

Jack Gilbert says, "We must unlearn the constellations to see the stars." Great writing doesn't show us new things; it shows us old things in new ways. How to achieve this? Close observation helps.

Examples
As the saw teeth bit down, the wood released its smell, each kind with its own fragrance, oak or walnut or cherry or pine—usually pine because it was the softest, easiest for a child to work. No matter how weathered or gray the board, no matter how warped and cracked, inside there was this smell waiting, as of something freshly baked.
    Scott Russell Sanders, "The Inheritance of Tools"

He took back his papers with careful hands, in which the papers shivered. The hands were ivory-coloured, the skin finely wrinkled everywhere, like the crust on a pool of wax, and under it appeared livid bruises, arthritic nodes, irregular tea-brown stains. William watched the hands fold the wavering papers and was filled with pity for them, as for sick and dying creatures. The flesh under the horny nails was candlewax-coloured, and bloodless.
    A.S. Byatt, "Morpho Eugenia"

Practice
A. Scientists tell us there are five types of taste: sweet, sour, bitter, salty, and umami (savory/meaty). Practice your observation of taste by writing a scene about a meal. Describe the food, a particular dish, or the whole meal. Have those partaking in the meal interact, using the food as the topic of discussion. Be specific.

B. Write a scene about someone outside late at night. It can be from memory or imagination. Evoke specifically at least three of the five senses.

See Additional Exercises: X1, X8, X16, X19, X29, X35, X38

OPENINGS

Readers are fickle and a strong opening is vital. That said, you don't want to promise something then not deliver. The best opening engages the story's central concern while also showing a command of language. Think analytically about what type of opening is best. Consider these four strategies:

1) The "W's" opening – stating up front **who** and **what** the piece is about, **where** and **when** it takes place, and sometimes even **why** it was written.

2) The *in media res* (in the middle of the action) opening – jumping right into the middle of a scene and engaging your reader with action and dialogue that might not make immediate sense but will resolve within a few paragraphs into a comprehensible storyline.

3) Setting – similar to an establishing shot in film, this type of opening uses a description of the setting to orient the reader to the place where at least some of the action will occur.

4) The meditative opening – ruminating on an idea or memory in a way that engages the reader immediately in the character's or narrator's thoughts.

By no means is this list exhaustive, but one thing good openings share is intentionality, the promise that a good story is unfolding.

Examples
1) W's – "In 1960, on one of the hottest June days on record, I went with my family to watch the Grand Floral Parade of Portland's annual Rose Festival." –David James Duncan, "Rose Vegetables"

2) *In media res* – "Long Tongue, The Blues Merchant, strolls on stage. His guitar rides sidesaddle against his hip." –Jerome Washington, "The Blues Merchant"

3) Setting – "This is where Scotland's dream was dashed. Windswept moor, purple with blooming heather. Bog land. Our shoes keep sinking into watery peat." –Judith Kitchen, "Culloden"

4) Meditative – "George Orwell wrote an essay called 'How the Poor Die' about his experience in the public ward of a Paris hospital during his lean years. I happened to read it not long ago…" –Tobias Wolff, "Last Shot"

See Additional Exercises: X6, X11, X12, X14, X15, X40

My instinct tells me that at the end of a story or a novel, I must artfully concentrate for the reader an impression of the entire work, and therefore must casually mention something about those whom I have already presented.

ANTON CHEKHOV

ENDINGS AND POWER POINTS

Hitchcock supposedly had every aspect of his films so closely thought out that he claimed the actual filming of them was tedious. It'd certainly be nice not to touch a pen to paper until the ending is known; however, more often than not, the writer doesn't have that luxury. We have to write into the unknown until we discover the ending, and only then can we return to the earlier parts and shape them so that the piece works as a complete and efficient whole.

That said, written narratives have several endings—to sentences, paragraphs, and sections—and each ending presents an opportunity. Good writers are attuned to these power points. Two especially prominent power points that occur in every prose piece include: 1) the end of the first paragraph; and 2) the very last word of the piece.

W.B. Yeats famously said that "a poem comes right with a click like a closing box." In prose this happens most often with something concrete. Debra Spark says, "When we think of effective closings, we think of a resonant final image or a powerful thought or a 'killer' line. Or we think of some combination of these three."

Examples
And still the warm round peach pie and the cool yellow cream we ate together that August night live in our hearts' palates, succulent, secret, delicious.
    M.F.K. Fisher, "A Thing Shared"

And it seemed as though in a little while the solution would be found, and then a new and splendid life would begin; and it was clear to both of them that they had still a long, long road before them, and that the most complicated and difficult part was only just beginning.
    Chekhov, "The Lady with the Dog"

Practice
A. Look at Fisher's example above. Here, she refers back to an important sensory image—eating a peach pie with her father— developed earlier in the piece. Freewrite an ending to something you're working on by hearkening back to a sensory image from earlier in it.

See Additional Exercises: X19, X21, X37

*The writer's characters must stand before us with a wonderful
clarity, such continuous clarity that nothing they do strikes us as
improbable behavior for just that character.*

JOHN GARDNER

CHARACTER APPEARANCE

The most basic tool of characterization is character appearance. Margot Livesey
complains that she has difficulty getting her characters to be more than a hair
color and a style of dress. She argues that a character's appearance must also
convey *attitude.* How a character looks should demonstrate something about
how she views the world.

Consider, too, E.M. Forster's concept of flat and round characters: "The test of a
round character is whether it is capable of surprising in a convincing way. If it
never surprises, it is flat. If it does not convince, it is flat pretending to be
round." To achieve a convincing and surprising character portrait, practice
overwriting your character's appearance to find those few necessary details that
are vivid and memorable and reveal something significant about her. Often it's a
single detail that's most striking.

Examples
Brother Charles was a big man in his early fifties with a full head of dark hair
and hands the size of waffle irons.
   Dennis Covington, *Salvation on Sand Mountain*

Everything about DeeDee spelled city, from her pearl rings to her hair tinted
increasingly dark shades every visit, sprayed at the roots so that it stood up
before fanning down around her heart-shaped face. I suspected that she made
her hair erect like that to give herself another inch or two. She always walked in
spike heels, never tottering, and the muscles in her calves bulged from her
breakneck strides. Pulled over that muscle, her skin was white, almost
transparent, and sometimes she wore shimmery nylons.
   Joy Passanante, *My Mother's Lovers*

Practice
A. Describe a character. Focus on striking details, specifics about how she
   looks, smells, feels, sounds. Evoke not only the colors of what she's wearing
   and her skin and hair, but also the texture of her skin, the sound of her voice.
   Fill a page with description.

B. Write a paragraph on the salient aspects of a character's personality—is he,
   in general, moody, happy, belligerent? Then write a second paragraph of
   description that captures these abstract aspects in bodily features—e.g., the
   appearance of his face, eyes, hands, shoulders, etc.

See Additional Exercises: X8, X23, X33, X38; Projects I, M

The character must do to the reader what he has done to the novelist—magnetize towards himself perceptions, sense-impressions, desires.

ELIZABETH BOWEN

CHARACTER BACKSTORY

Information about a character's (or narrator's) past is called backstory and can be incorporated into an advancing storyline either through summary or flashback. Summary may cover a large amount of time—months, years, decades —versus a flashback, which is a scene grounded in a particular past moment.

When we know a person's history, we become more sympathetic or at least interested in her present and future. Thus, backstory is vital for connecting a character (or yourself, if writing nonfiction) to the reader. Using backstory in a way that's organic is the key.

Example
Ten pigeons pick up the remaining crumbs left by their patron. A sudden flap of wings, they rise, bank, and return...
And then I remember standing on the edge of Great Salt Lake as a young girl, watching hundreds and thousands of birds fly over me, feeling the wind of wings, the songs of a world in motion.
    Terry Tempest Williams, *Leap*

First, he felt a tremendous elation. Grigoriev was lying there, not him...Second was the sweet, pungent odor of disinfectant. Never had Yuri perceived such a perfectly disinfecting scent. His body was cleansed just inhaling it. Although the odor was nothing like Gzhatsk, it evoked his hometown and the quiet, shrubbery-lined lane that passed behind the house and meandered to school. He recalled the apple and cherry trees and the bushes thick with gooseberries and currants. The odor of the disinfectant was the chemical distillation of Russia, lush and confident, marching ahead to the future.
    Ken Kalfus, "Orbit"

Practice
A. Here's an exercise from Tom Bailey's *On Writing Short Stories* (p. 65) that can be used to generate a story or an essay that will incorporate backstory. "Write a short unified piece...which begins with a summary and then shifts into the forward motion of a direct scene, [then] makes a seamless transition that carries us into a pertinent flashback." Finish by returning to the direct scene and finding an important moment on which to end.

See Additional Exercises: X4, X5, X23, X25, X29, X34; Projects G, K

SKETCHING A CROWD

Bringing to life many people at once on the page—or, sketching a crowd, as I call it—can be difficult, especially in a short space. One way, as in the Cummins example below, is to generalize about types of people. Another way, as in the Doerr example, is to survey a few individuals for a representative "flavor." With either method, the details must convince the reader through distinction and revelation.

Remember, too, that the purpose of crowd sketching is to characterize the *place* that they're found—i.e., sketching a crowd is part of the setting. Therefore, choose characters who fit the place but also exhibit some striking or surprising aspect.

Examples
At Pope John Paul's Funeral on St. Peter's Square:
A woman pushes through the crowd, head down, wildflowers in both fists. Beside me a teenager with strands of barbed wire tattooed around his wrists wipes his eyes with the hem of his shirt. A nun on a suitcase gives me a smile.
    Anthony Doerr, *Four Seasons in Rome*

He hits the Albuquerque city limits just before sundown. Driving up Central, he sees a lot of tired drunks sitting on the low stone wall that edges the university and a lot of college girls in short shorts walking on the sidewalks. Hippies in long skirts and bra tops hug up against long-haired white boys and dreadlocked black guys, all drinking juice at the juice shop. Cowboys in hats and shades walk too carefully down the street, heel to toe, as if they have to concentrate— these are probably rodeo boys with sore bones, looking for bars.
    Ann Cummins, *Yellowcake*

Practice
A. Work on a piece of your writing in which you describe a crowd. Sketch the crowd by focusing on a handful of memorable figures. Describe them in detail, overwriting their description at first. Try to capture the essence of the place in your descriptions of its people. Evoke motion and personality.

B. Take an imaginary stroll down the main street of your hometown, describing the people you pass. Try to capture mood and atmosphere through the characters' appearances.

C. Revise either A or B above by winnowing down your descriptions to include only the barest, most evocative details.

See Additional Exercises: X39

Surprise is the very basis of art.

DEBRA SPARK

SURPRISE

"No surprise for the writer, no surprise for the reader," Robert Frost famously said. Life delivers the unexpected, so why shouldn't good writing? "The best work I do comes out of the ways in which I'm surprised while I'm writing," says Tobias Wolff.

The inevitable surprise is the artistic ideal. When a reader encounters something in a narrative that's both shocking and unavoidable (though the unavoidable aspect ideally appears only in retrospect), she becomes complicit with the text. The surprise that accords both convinces her of the story's value and invests her more deeply in its unfolding.

Surprise also delights the reader because it's built on trust. The writer trusts the reader to make the connections necessary to incorporate the surprise into all that's come before.

Examples
"You, my daughter, have the gift of healing. You are a healer!" Behind me the praise grew louder. The room felt suddenly hot and I wished for an open door, a window letting in the cool night air. [The preacher's] hands were heavier than my legs could stand and I fell, sweat trickling down my sides.
   Kim Barnes, *In the Wilderness*

He kissed her then, on the lips, for real; he came for her in a kind of lunging motion and practically poured his tongue down her throat. It was a terrible kiss, shockingly bad; Margot had trouble believing that a grown man could possibly be so bad at kissing. It seemed awful, yet somehow it also gave her that tender feeling toward him again, the sense that even though he was older than her, she knew something he didn't.
   Kristen Roupenian, "Cat Person"

Practice
A. Make a list of five times you or one of your characters was surprised. Choose one and write about it. Develop or extend a scene around the surprise.

B. Practice writing surprise from interiority—that is, plumb the depths of thought. If nonfiction, use your own thoughts, and if fiction, access a character's thoughts. Begin with the phrase, "In that moment, I was surprised to find that I felt…" and explore. Don't try to force a narrative. Instead, follow your intuition. Be alert for unexpected emotions.

When you think the idea is just right, when the character is exactly what you want her to be, exaggerate an aspect of her that nobody else has ever thought of exaggerating. Or give the character a little twist.

ORSON SCOTT CARD

REVERSALS

In fiction writing, one way to build in surprise for a reader is to practice reversals. Try, when writing a scene, to project what happens next, then do its *opposite*.

For example, Orson Scott Card tells of drafting a story about a young king who was required to abstain from sex at the risk of causing his kingdom to collapse. Card's first impulse was to make the young king constantly yearning to escape his guardians. Another writer, Gene Wolfe, pointed out a more realistic trait that *reverses* this cliché expectation: "No, no you don't understand. This young man thinks they don't restrict him *enough*. He's absolutely terrified that he'll accidentally slip into some form of sexual release and cause some dire consequence to his people. He'd make sure they watch him all the time." In this way, reversing expectations creates a more believable interior conflict within the young king.

Especially for nonfiction, the application is to be alert to inner reversals, that is, emotional states being overturned or contradicted.

Example
Along with sadness, a sense of relief followed my father's death. At least we weren't waiting anymore. Also we were going to receive some money from the insurance…I was sitting in the kitchen a couple of days after my dad's funeral. Perhaps we were still in shock, but Sarah and I were laughing hysterically over a new joke we'd heard.
Lucy Grealy, *Autobiography of a Face*

The man with the pistol walked over to Anders. He poked the weapon into Anders' gut. "You think I'm playing games?"
"No," Anders said, but the barrel tickled like a stiff finger and he had to fight back the titters.
Tobias Wolff, "Bullet in the Brain"

Practice
A. Choose a reversal-based scenario and develop it: 1) a man who's happy to get into a car wreck; 2) a person who dislikes happiness; 3) a mother who's decided she doesn't love her children; 4) someone who enjoys standing in lines.

B. Describe a time in your life when your own reaction surprised you. When did you express great poise, fear, or anger?

*We were here; we are human beings; this is how we lived. Let it be
known, the earth passed before us. Our details are important.
Otherwise, if they are not, we can drop a bomb and it doesn't matter.*

NATALIE GOLDBERG

SETTING

Seeing a character in a specific place helps a reader picture scenes more clearly.
Nailing down the setting is vital to create the "dream" in which the work exists.
Settings are best evoked through sensory detail, and to make them three-
dimensional, incorporate appeals to at least three of the five senses.

Examples
The entire apartment was a Santería shrine: cigars laid across the tops of glasses
of colorless liquid; open scissors on dishes of blue liquid; dried black bananas
hanging over the threshold; Tarot cards, coins, and dice before a dozen statues of
saints, including a huge Virgin Mary with a triple-headed angel at her feet.
    Marcus Laffey, "The Midnight Tour"

At the fairgrounds we saw them in the parking lot inhaling the effluvium of
carnival, the smells of fried dough, caramel and cinnamon, the flap-flapping of
tents, a carousel plinking out music-box songs, voluptuous sounds bouncing
down tent ropes and along the trampled dust of the midway. Wind-curled
handbills staple-gunned to telephone poles, the hum of gas-powered generators
and the gyro truck, the lemonade truck, pretzels and popcorn, baked potatoes,
the American flag, the rumblings of rides and the disconnected screams of riders
—all of it shimmered before them like a mirage, something not quite real.
    Anthony Doerr, "For a Long Time This Was Griselda's Story"

Exercise
A. Consider a piece of your writing that needs a setting. Describe the setting by
capturing its details. Don't assume anything is too small to jot down—you
can always cut it later.

B. Drill down into a setting on which you're working. First, describe the
surface landforms, then go down into the soil. This will likely require
research. What type of soil is it and where did it come from? What roots
grow there and what fossils can be found in it? What mineral deposits exist?
What is in the earth on which this place sits?

C. Revise a scene from something you're working on in an anti-naturalist way.
Naturalism reflects the character's inner state in the outer world, so a happy
character might look out onto a glorious sunset. Try doing the opposite;
instead of reflecting the character's interior, make the setting at odds with it.

See Additional Exercises: X2, X16, X17, X20

Chiefly, the novelist must control his infatuation with his own visual power. No non-contributory image, must be the rule. Contributory to what? To the mood of the 'now,' the mood that either projects or reflects action.

ELIZABETH BOWEN

SETTING VS. EVOCATION

Description falls short of evocation. A page of description about a mountain can be deadening, but a page of evocation not only brings the mountain to life, it also enlivens characters, metaphors, and thematic lines. By using vivid sense images, you activate your reader's imagination and control the images that appear there.

Examples
Just a month before the onset of my illness, I had visited the Guggenheim Museum in New York. Halfway down the rotunda's spiraling interior, I stopped. It was dizzying to look up as the floors curved around and above me and equally so to look down to the ground level far below. Now I tried to imagine, were I as large in proportion to the Guggenheim as the snail to its shell, what it would be like to have my head stick out the main entrance below and my body wind all the way up the spiraling floor.
    Elisabeth Tova Bailey, *The Sound of a Wild Snail Eating*

They descended the mountain, going down over the rocks with their hands outheld before them and their shadows contorted on the broken terrain like creatures seeking their own forms. They reached the valley floor at dusk and set off across the blue and cooling land, the mountains to the west a line of jagged slate set endwise in the earth and the dry weeds heeling and twisting in a wind sprung from nowhere.
    Cormac McCarthy, *Blood Meridian*

Practice
A. From Priscilla Long's *The Writer's Portable Mentor*: "Describe a room of your house from the point of view of someone who is totally depressed, has lost the love of his life, his money…his job, etc. Do not mention any of these circumstances. Only describe the room. Now describe the same exact room again, from the point of view of a happy person."

B. Exaggerate part of your present mood and, through that intentionally distorted lens, describe the place where you are now. Capture details but do so through a filter of feeling.

See Additional Exercises: X12, X18, X19, X26, X39

If you are using dialogue—say it aloud as you write it. Only then will it have the sound of speech.

JOHN STEINBECK

DIALOGUE

Jesse Lee Kercheval offers this dialogue advice: "Every line must be both interesting and either add to your readers' understanding of your character or help establish a sense of place or advance the plot. The best dialogue works overtime to do all these things at once."

Dialogue is only a representation of real speech. Tape-recorded conversations run to great length and often have no point. In good prose, however, dialogue is extremely shaped and it typically comes in revelatory bursts.

Economy is the trick. At first, overwrite dialogue using freewrites, then jettison all the fillers—the greetings and niceties, the lines that exude no energy. Summarize the bulk of the conversation, then keep in dialogue only the most evocative, personality-laden phrases.

Examples
And my mother was standing in the back whispering loudly, "Why he don't send me check, already two weeks late. So mad he lie to me, losing me money." And then I said in perfect English, "Yes, I'm getting rather concerned. You had agreed to send the check two weeks ago, but it hasn't arrived."
Then she began to talk more loudly. "What he want, I come to New York tell him front of his boss, you cheating me?"
    Amy Tan, "Mother Tongue"

Hit the Escape key. Look, all you have to do is this and this.
You go so fast, she said. Would you like some coffee?
He eyed her briefly. I don't drink coffee.
Tea?
What kind of tea?
    Janet Burroway, "Tea Leaves"

Practice
A. Write "rants" for two characters on two different subjects (e.g., airport security, turn signals, etc.). Then combine the rants into a single conversation, altering them as necessary.

B. Create a situation or recall a conversation in which one speaker desperately wants something from another speaker who doesn't want to give it. Capture this dynamic in a page of dialogue.

See Additional Exercises: X40; Project L

Beats enable your readers to picture the action in a scene, allow you to vary the rhythm of the dialogue, and help reveal your characters' personalities.

RENNI BROWNE AND DAVE KING

BEATS

Beats are the tidbits of setting or gesture or thought that occur between passages of dialogue. They act as a pause between speaking and create a verisimilitude that helps bring the scene to life in the reader's mind.

A general rule of thumb is that if the scene has high situational tension, few beats are necessary, whereas in a scene with low tension, more beats can increase its interest and pull the reader along. The best beats are fresh and unique to the character.

Examples
"Now what it is, son," said Uncle Alton, when he had everything ready, "is he's crawbound. Feel right here." He took my hand and put it at the base of the rooster's neck. As young as I was, I had felt enough chicken's craws to know something was wrong. The rooster's was tight and solid as stone. "He'll be dead in a few days, maybe even tomorrow if we don't help'm. We got to clean out that craw."

Harry Crews, *A Childhood*

"What's your name? I never got your name."
"Belle Starr," she said, and, winking at him, she made a clicking sound out of the side of her mouth.
"Belle Starr," he said.
"Don't you know who Belle Starr was?"
All he knew was that it was a familiar-sounding name. "Belle Starr."
She put her index finger to the side of his head and said, "Bang."

Richard Bausch, "The Man Who Knew Belle Starr"

Practice
A. Write a short scene with dialogue two different ways.
   1) First, write it with only dialogue tags—"he said," "she said," etc.
   2) Then rewrite it, inserting beats after each person speaks. Give them a gesture, a thought, a flash of recognition, or include a setting or character detail. Intentionally overwrite the beats at first, allowing them to change the dialogue if it does so naturally.
   3) Finally, draft the scene a third way, choosing the best pieces from both previous drafts to form an organic and economical whole.

See Additional Exercises: X9, X40

Of all the qualities, voice is the most unteachable and the closest to magic, a sort of natural music in the head.

BARRY HANNAH

VOICE

Voice can be divided into four components:
1) Dialect - place infusing the voice with an accent
2) Attitude - personality or mood inflecting the voice
3) Diction - particular words spicing the voice with slang, lingo, or a sense of social class
4) Tone - the surfacing of the author's attitude toward her work

In fiction, the writer can assume a character's voice; in nonfiction, the writer assumes the voice of a persona. *All* of it is artifice, performance on the page. To attain the natural sound of a voice, follow your intuition and improvise as you go. If you can clearly hear a line or two from a distinctive voice in your head, that can be a great place to start. If not, freewrite until a voice suggests itself.

Examples
We live entirely, especially if we are writers, by the imposition of a narrative line upon disparate images, by the "ideas" with which we have learned to freeze the shifting phantasmagoria which is our actual experience.
    Or at least we do for a while. I am talking here about a time when I began to doubt the premises of all the stories I had ever told myself, a common condition but one I found troubling.
    Joan Didion, "The White Album"

He looked like a drownded puppy, in them overalls, without no hat, splashed up to his knees where he had walked them four miles in the mud.
    William Faulkner, *As I Lay Dying*

Practice
A. Capture in writing a voice that speaks with great authority. To begin, give yourself 3 or 4 minutes just to ruminate or freewrite, seeking to find a voice that speaks with great authority on some subject. Once you can hear a line spoken clearly by that voice in your mind's ear, simply record what you hear. Follow the voice wherever it goes.

B. Follow the process above in A, but this time try to capture the voice of someone who's lying. If you're practicing nonfiction, start by telling a lie yourself. Again, ruminate until you hear the lie clearly in your head, then simply follow and record.

See Additional Exercises: X22, X27, X32

Writers live twice.

NATALIE GOLDBERG

USING MEMORY

Memories are the writer's storehouse. Francois Camoin, in "Writing the Story," says this about memory and writing:

> The way you keep your life in the garage, stacked up in haphazard piles, and when you need to fill a hole in a story you fumble through the wreckage, hold up something to the light—a gray meal eaten in Gallup, New Mexico, the time when your ex-wife broke your finger with a metal chair-leg and you duct-taped yourself together for a month until it healed, a fig-tree on Anacapa Street, a particularly bad Christmas, a bicycle you repainted a weird color, your mother's death—hold it up to the light, sight down the edge to see if it's too warped to be useful, sand it a little and glue it into place.

Example
Not that I was ever afraid of fire, exactly. As a boy, I was as much a pyromaniac as any of my friends, perhaps more so. I was fascinated with the burn barrel. After all, fire and I knew each other intimately.

   Robert Coker Johnson, "What I Know of Fire"

I could write quite a lot about the Czechs in the French army: the 11,000 soldiers, made up of 3,000 volunteers and 8,000 expatriate Czech conscripts, along with the brave pilots, trained at Chartres, who will shoot down or help to shoot down more than 130 enemy planes during the Battle of France…But I've said that I don't want to write a historical handbook. This story is personal. That's why my vision sometimes gets mixed up with the known facts. It's just how it is.

   Laurent Binet, *HHhh*

Practice
A. Taking a minute for each item, write the first memories that come to mind when you consider each of these ten things: grass; insect; cloud; house; family; board game; friend; liquid; car; school. Now choose one especially evocative memory from those to flesh out in a full-page description or scene.

B. Think of a place that holds significant memories. Draw a map of that place and label not only its physical landmarks but its emotional ones, too. Then zoom in on details and describe them specifically as you move through the place.

C. In his memoir, *Speak, Memory*, Nabokov writes, "In our childhood we know a lot about hands since they live and hover at the level of our stature." What hands do you recall from childhood? Write about them.

See Additional Exercises: X1, X2, X4, X5, X7, X9, X25, X29; Projects G, H

When the action is hot, write cool.

DEBRA JORGE

WRITING VIOLENCE

Nothing turns off the reader faster than a violent scene mishandled. Often the best choice is to keep the violence off-page and focus on its repercussions instead. Sometimes, though, we need to see the moment of violence. Of this, Flannery O'Connor says, "I have found that violence is strangely capable of returning my characters to reality and preparing them to accept their moment of grace. Their heads are so hard that almost nothing else will do the work."

A common error in writing violence is overdoing it by bombarding the reader with gory B-movie-grade descriptions. The better choice is to minimize the details and focus on powerful verbs. Aim for the least amount of violence that maintains the greatest menace or impact, and avoid labeling the violence (e.g. "murder").

Imagine a woman named Harriett witnessing her husband Jack as he's shot by an escaped convict beside the road:

Overwritten example
Harriett watched in horror as the convict raised the gun and blew a hole through Jack's chest. Blood exploded everywhere and Jack slumped limp and lifeless to the ground. A red pool of blood spread around the murdered man.

What's wrong with this scene?
* an overuse of adjectives and adverbs *tells* the reader what to feel and see instead of simply showing what happened
* word choice draws the reader's attention to the gore
* cliché details miscast the emotional effects on Harriett

Example
Then Robert Ford's .44 ignited and a red stamp seemed to paste against the outlaw's chestnut brown hair one inch to the rear of his right ear, and his left eyebrow socked into the glassed watercolor of Skyrocket. Gunpowder and gun noise filled the room and Jesse groaned as a man does in his sleep and then sagged from his knees and tilted over and smacked the floor like a great animal, shaking the house with his fall.
   Ron Hansen, *The Assassination of Jesse James...*

Practice
A. Write a scene that includes violence. Avoid titillation and shock by focusing on details that evoke the action vividly and directly. Use no adjectives; instead, use powerful verbs.

See Additional Exercise: X6, X31; Project O

Only trouble is interesting.

JANET BURROWAY

CREATING TENSION

Dramatic tension keeps the reader reading, and there are three primary types:

Narrative Tension arises from the story's structure and causes the reader to wonder, *What happens next?* "A novel, play, or any type of writing, really is a crisis from beginning to end growing to its necessary conclusion," says Lajos Egri. If the narrative tension is taut, the reader will feel compelled to see how things work out.

Internal Tension capitalizes on the struggles inside of a character (or yourself, if nonfiction). What are the secret forces—fears, expectations, and desires—at work within? What happens if the character or narrator fails to rise to the occasion? Internal tension appears when innermost thoughts are revealed.

Situational Tension appears when action and dialogue are detailed. It's the sense the reader gets that something important is happening, and it often derives its power from connections and disconnections between characters. A looming raincloud or a cigarette with a dangling column of ash can also build situational tension. In each scene, the reader should be engaged by moment-to-moment sensory details that evoke the unpredictability of time moving forward. Physical or emotional menace further amplifies situational tension.

Example - Narrative Tension
We decided to shoot the cat on the third Sunday in May, the day our home church in North Carolina celebrates Memorial Day. My family was sitting together on the front porch of my grandmother's house. We had been to church.
    Tony Earley, "Shooting the Cat"

People do not give it credence that a fourteen-year-old girl could leave home and go off in the wintertime to avenge her father's blood but it did not seem so strange then, although I will say it did not happen every day.
    Charles Portis, *True Grit*

Example - Internal Tension
I think about the kiss all the time, but each time I consider asking my father about it, I find I can't open my mouth. It's not just that I'm afraid he might tell me what I don't want to hear, but that I'm so thoroughly under the spell of my own denial I sometimes wonder if anything happened at all.
    Kathryn Harrison, *The Kiss*

Peering over the edge of the limestone cavity, I have an otherworldly certainty that I have been here before. It's one of those rare moments, the air thick and perfumed with memory, when the imagined world and the real world seem to overlap. A catatonic calm takes hold of me. *Oh, no,* I think, staring into the swirling, milky center, the blind eye of the sinkhole. We should not be doing this.

> Karen Russell, "Z. Z.'s Sleep-Away Camp…"

Example - Situational Tension
The weasel was stunned into stillness as he was emerging from beneath an enormous shaggy wild rose bush four feet away. I was stunned into stillness twisted backward on the tree trunk. Our eyes locked, and someone threw away the key.

> Annie Dillard, "Living Like Weasels"

She feels his fingers at the back of her dress and—steeling herself with a deep breath—manages,
"Please don't do that."
Ward steps back, suddenly full of reserve, worried.
"It's not that, Mister Ward," she says. "Unless you can fix it yourself, you'd better leave it as is."
"All right," he says. He steps closer and puts his hands on her shoulders. "Am I offending you?"
"Not at all," she says.
"Then call me Herbert."
"I really can't do that," she says. "And don't call me Sarita, but think it. Think it all the time."

> Sabina Murray, *Valiant Gentlemen*

Practice
A. Sketch the narrative tension for a new piece. On a sheet of paper turned to landscape orientation, draw an arc across the top. Using the arc as the piece's backbone, label the narrative's major occurrences or realizations that will keep the reader reading.

B. Practice writing internal tension. Reflect (or have a character reflect) on a moment of deep uncertainty about something important. Really try to recapture your (or your character's) moment-to-moment thoughts during that crisis.

C. Write a scene with high situational tension. Think of a time when you were in imminent danger. Depending on whether you're working with nonfiction or fiction, reconstruct the memory accordingly by detailing and/or embellishing the scene.

See Additional Exercises: X9, X12, X14, X26, X35, X36; Projects B, I, K

The title is the window through which the reader crawls like a burglar.

ROBERT WRIGLEY

CHOOSING A TITLE

When casting about for a title after finishing a book, Hemingway claimed that he listed sometimes as many as a hundred possibilities. Then one-by-one he would eliminate them, keeping the best.

Because a title stands detached from the work itself, it presents a unique opportunity for the writer to comment on the work from outside of it. When Salinger titles his novel *The Catcher in the Rye*, he thereby points to the significance of a particular scene in Chapter 22 when his protagonist Holden Caulfield reveals his dream of standing in a field of rye and catching children before they fall from a cliff. The image evokes Holden's desire to preserve innocence, and the title signals this concept's centrality.

The title is your first point of contact with the reader. As such it should provoke interest even as it creates in her mind a new, inviting place. The ideal title is sonically pleasant and memorable.

One-Word Titles

1984	Night
Persuasion	Waiting
House	Rain
Beloved	Divorcer
Swamplandia!	1Q84
Disgrace	Balboa
Amerika	Infidel

Other Titles

Of Cannibals	Total Eclipse
Everything that Rises Must Converge	Slouching Towards Bethlehem
I Stand Here Ironing	Consider the Lobster
The Knife Thrower	The Boys of My Youth
	The Safety of Objects

Practice

A. Make a list of several one-word titles for a piece you're working on or have finished. Start with the most obvious, then branch out.

B. List titles for one of your pieces that capture sensory experience—sight, smell, taste, touch, sound—described in the work.

C. Take an existing title or familiar saying and riff on it for the title of a piece you're working on. List several.

In the whole composition there should be no word written, of which the tendency, direct or indirect, is not to the one pre-established design.

EDGAR ALLEN POE

PROFLUENCE

For this theme, first do part of the practice.

Practice, Part 1

A. Write a definition of the short story or the essay (depending on the genre in which you're currently working). Consider what it must have, at minimum, to be defined as such.

B. Write a second definition. This time, define what makes a "good" short story or essay.

The reader reads for cause-and-effect. You'll often hear readers talk about how well a piece "flows," but "flow" is an indistinct and unhelpful term. A more specific and useful term is profluence.

John Gardner applied the term profluence (from the Latin *prōfluentia*, or fluency in speech) to written narrative. In *The Art of Fiction*, he describes how profluence acts on the reader: "Page 1, even if it's a page of description, raises questions, suspicions, and expectations; the mind casts forward to later pages, wondering what will come about and how. It is this casting forward that draws us from paragraph to paragraph and chapter to chapter."

In a blog post, Ingrid Sundberg writes, "Profluence is the cause-and-effect connective tissue that constructs the flow of time in the story world, as well as the underlying engine that makes the novel coherent to the reader."

Profluence requires your narrative to have nothing superfluous, a state achieved, most often, through intense revision.

Practice, Part 2

C. "The moment we stop caring where the story will go next, the writer has failed," says Gardner. Write reflectively about a piece you're working on, considering its profluence. You might start by describing its event-sequence —that is, its cause-and-effect. Are there any scenes that need to be added to clarify how events are linked? In other words, can the reader follow the progression of what happens, and why, throughout? Alternatively, are there any parts that can be cut without harming the overall coherence?

D. Revisit your definitions in A and B. What changes would you make; and if none, why not?

See Additional Exercises: X6, X10, X26, X37; Projects B, N

PART II

LANGUAGE WORK

The specificity of our art is how we reach for universality.

RICHARD RODRIGUEZ

SENSE IMAGES: CONCRETE VS. ABSTRACT

Everything we know about the world comes to us through our five senses. William Carlos Williams states this when he writes, "No idea, but in things." Great writing is grounded in concrete, sensory language. **Concrete words** are those perceived through a sense organ: eyes, ears, skin, tongue, nose. You can always specify *which* sense organ has perceived: yellow (eyes), rotten eggs (nose), or feather-soft (skin). **Abstract words**, like "love" or "inscrutable" or "freedom," cannot be perceived through any sense organ.

There's another aspect to using concrete language. It connects us to the world. Natalie Goldberg says, "Give things the dignity of their names." In other words, don't write "car," write, "1966 Pontiac GTO." Not "tree" but "hornbeam maple." Doing so forces us to know the things in front of us, to engage with our surroundings.

Examples
Botany cannot go farther than tell me the names of the shrubs which grow there, —the high-blueberry, panicled andromeda, lamb-kill, azalea, and rhodora,—all standing in the quaking sphagnum.
    Henry Thoreau, "Walking"

Whale is blasting rust out of a tight spot behind a tie brace, and Baby moves in to spray primer one, when suddenly his paint gun sputters and dies. He yanks off his noise helmet, shouts at Whale over the wind, and unclips his safety line to go look for the kink in his paint hose.
    Daniel Orozco, "The Bridge"

Practice
A. Make a list of all the jobs you've had, paid and unpaid. Choose one and make another running list of all the concrete words associated with that job. It may include the people who worked there, too. Write a scene using this concrete-word list. Try to appeal to all five senses.

B. Thoreau writes, "[I]n wildness is the preservation of the world." Using his belief in wildness as our vital source for inspiration, take a walk outside— the more wild the place, the better. After, record your impressions as concretely as possible.

See Additional Exercises: X1, X16, X17, X25, X26; Projects A, F

The storyteller must use the visible, the physical, the eminently tangible: the reader, first and foremost, must be convinced. And details—the right details in the right places—are what do the convincing.

ANTHONY DOERR

LEVELS OF CONCRETION

A "Three Little Pigs" analogy: some language is straw and easily blows away from the reader's mind; some is wooden and withstands better; the best is brick and cannot be blown away.

For example: "couch" is straw language, vague and hard to remember; "red velvet couch" is clearer and will last longer in memory; "tomato-red leather loveseat with armrests worn to a sheen and coffee stains on the cushions" is brick language—not an image that will readily disappear.

You'll find that you often don't know the specific names for things. First, simply record in detail all that you can—"a fat-bellied bird with a funny feather sticking out of its head that scampers and rarely flies but calls *er-att-err*;" and later, track down the correct name—"California quail."

Become a collector of such specifics. Find books on the flora and fauna of the region about which you write. Visit websites and peruse the "local" sections of bookstores. Of course, not every image needs to be described at the level of brick language, but doing so signifies the importance of the object being described and makes the narrative's world more vivid.

Examples
The man would set off late in the spring, after the dogwood had bloomed, in the blue '58 Chevy pickup with the broken taillight and the cracked Expando mirrors.
    Barry Lopez, "The Hot Spring"

Her father radiates a thousand colors, opal, strawberry red, deep russet, wild green; a smell like oil and metal, the feel of a lock tumbler sliding home, the sound of his key rings chiming as he walks.
    Anthony Doerr, *All the Light We Cannot See*

Practice
A. Choose an object with which you're familiar. Describe it at three different levels: straw, wooden, and brick. When might each be best?

See Additional Exercises: X2, X16, X17, X35; Project H

A simple observation: superb writers write list sentences. Average writers don't.

PRISCILLA LONG

LIST SENTENCES

List sentences lend authority and specificity to your writing. They make sentences more interesting for the reader, and they catalog the story's world, providing proof of its authenticity.

Lists are often nouns, but consider expanding other parts of the sentence—verbs, adjectives, adverbs. Play with the rhythm of the list; find its most melodic order.

Examples
All other fields of study simply use the intervals of time known to us all: seconds, minutes, hours, days, and so on. Geologists, on the other hand, talk about periods and epochs, eras and zones, stages and series, the arcane subdivisions of what is known as the geological timescale.
  Peter Ward, *Gorgon*

To kill is to put to death, extinguish, nullify, cancel, destroy. But from the hunter's point of view, it's just a tiny part of the Experience.
  Joy Williams, "The Killing Game"

The rifleman did not, does not, will not, understand the ramifications. He reasoned that since the trespassers outnumbered him, he had a right to defend his property, his stronghold.
  Jen Hirt, "Stronghold"

Her face slips into the light to kiss and lick and taste.
  Michael Ondaatje, *The English Patient*

Practice
A. Take a simple subject-verb-object sentence from your writing, like "The man walked down the road." Then expand, separately, each part of the sentence: first subject, then verb, then object. Work toward making the image as arresting as possible. (E.g., a subject expansion might look like, "The man—the outcast, the criminal, the person who would become my father—walked down the road.")

B. Create a character by cataloging their traits. Use list sentences.

C. Describe a room using only list sentences.

See Additional Exercises: X20

We touch a sphere, see a small heap of dawn-colored light, our mouths enjoy a tingling sensation, and we lie to ourselves that those three disparate things are only one thing called an orange.

JORGE LUIS BORGES

DEFAMILIARIZATION

When we become habituated to the familiar, we begin to lose feeling. This happens in language. For instance, here are some clichés: on top of the world, hot as hell, pain in the neck. Do these make you feel anything sensorily? Probably not.

According to Viktor Shklovsky, clichés occur when language becomes automatized. The problem, he writes, is that "automatization eats away at things, at clothes, at furniture, at one's wife, and at our fear of war." In other words, overuse and familiarity breed loss of feeling. To counter this, we're given the tool of art. We can defamiliarize—that is, remove an image from its typical associations—by describing it in fresh, imaginative ways.

Examples
…she saw giant flying sharks with lateral eyes taking barely one night to carry pilgrims through black ether across an entire continent from dark to shining sea, before booming back to Seattle or Wark.
　　Vladimir Nabokov, *Ada* [a description of airplanes]

She had to make a supernatural effort not to die when a startlingly regulated cyclonic power lifted her up by the waist and despoiled her of her intimacy with three slashes of its claws and quartered her like a little bird. She managed to thank God for having been born before she lost herself in the inconceivable pleasure of that unbearable pain, splashing in the steaming marsh of the hammock which absorbed the explosion of blood like a blotter.
　　Gabriel Garcia Marquez, *One Hundred Years of Solitude*

Practice
A. Defamiliarize each of these clichés by finding new descriptions that are true to the initial meaning but evoke it in a fresh way. Time yourself, spending no more than 2 minutes on each: stomach butterflies, pitch black, dry as a bone, cat got your tongue, raining cats and dogs, scared to death.

B. Freewrite a description of a common object. At first capture it using common phrases and clichés. Then push yourself to describe the item as if you're an archeologist from 1000 years in the future, discovering it with no idea of its purpose.

See Additional Exercises: X39; Project O

What do we need more, the world or its reflection?

AIMEE BENDER

IMAGERY

How does it happen? The eyes pass over tiny symbols preserved in ink, and the brain somehow conjures the sensation of biting into a hot, buttery ear of corn. To evoke sights, sounds, smells, tastes, and textures from black marks on the page is truly an amazing illusion.

Imagery is language that creates sensation. Images are the locus for the most intimate connection with the reader—that moment when a writer accurately paints, using the reader's triggered memories, a particular intended sensation.

"When is description mere? Never," said Theodore Roethke, and it's the poets who remind us that an image is most powerful when it's not only vivid but resonant with meaning. Create images that elevate the reader when they resolve. In other words, be specific but allow room for the reader's interpretive powers to do some work.

Examples
The city was a real city, shifty and sexual. I was lightly jostled by small herds of flushed young sailors looking for action on Forty-second Street, with its rows of X-rated movie houses, brassy women, glittering souvenir shops, and hot-dog vendors. I wandered through Kino parlors and peered through the windows of the magnificent sprawling Grant's Raw Bar filled with men in black coats scooping up piles of fresh oysters.
  Patti Smith, *Just Kids*

Within the miniature palace, which is no larger than a small table, one can see, by means of a magnifying lens, myriad pieces of precise furniture, as well as entire sets of cups, bowls, and dishes, and even a pair of scissors so tiny that when fully opened they can be concealed behind the leg of a fly.
  Steven Millhauser, "Cathay"

Practice
A. Taking 1 to 2 minutes for each, describe in quick succession the first sensory image that springs to mind from these prompts: a faded photograph, a powerful smell, a delicious taste, a rough texture, an odd sound.

B. Recall from childhood two powerful memories based around two different sense organs (e.g., sound and taste). Describe both scenes, then find a way to combine the two.

See Additional Exercises: X1, x18, X19, X21, X25, X26, X35; Project A

To make a rule "never use the same word twice in one paragraph,"
or to state flatly that repetition is to be avoided, is to throw away
one of the most valuable tools of narrative prose.

URSULA K. LE GUIN

REPETITION

Repetition is sometimes overlooked by prose writers as a tool, but it's an excellent way to signal significance to a reader. It can also lend a lyrical or humorous feel to the writing. Repetition is closely related to rhythm, and without a good ear the repetition will fall flat or sound awkward. One trick is to use the Rule of Three—repeating something twice. A single repetition can seem like a mistake, but repeating immediately, then once more signals intention and importance.

Examples
You've been waiting for a story to see how these things connect: you've been waiting for a reason why crows visited me one winter and why I paid them mind.
Robert Vivian, "The Dark Hangnails of God"

People look at the sky and at the other animals. They make beautiful objects, beautiful sounds, beautiful motions of their bodies beating drums in lines.
Annie Dillard, "This Is The Life"

These were simple people with simple beliefs, who simply wanted to be left to themselves.
Nathan Englander, "The Tumblers"

He was half sitting, half lying, propped up on his elbow facing her with the sky-blue sky of the sky behind him.
Toni Morrison, *Tar Baby*

Practice
A. Write a paragraph that repeats a word on every line. Make it a significant word, one with resonant meaning, and force the repetition. Then revise to make it sound more natural.

B. Write a paragraph that noticeably repeats three different significant words (not something like "and" or "is" or "the"). Read it aloud and see whether others hear the repeated words.

C. Write a paragraph in which you noticeably repeat a phrase or syntactical construction (e.g. "we came, we saw, we conquered"). Do it for effect, to reinforce and call attention to the phrase's importance.

Style is a very simple matter: it is all rhythm.

VIRGINIA WOOLF

RHYTHM

Most great prose writers are rhythm stylists, evoking the music in language. Listen to the rhythms in everyday speech. Sometimes it helps to refine a phrase while walking, using your footsteps to meter the line. Listening to music also trains your ear for language rhythms.

Examples
When the ancient light grey is clean it is yellow, it is a silver seller. This is a please this is a please there are the saids to jelly. These are the wets these say the sets to leave a crown to Incy.
Incy is short for incubus.
A pot. A pot is a beginning of a rare bit of trees.
Trees tremble, the old vats are in bobbles, bobbles which shade and shove and render clean, render clean must.
    Gertrude Stein, "Susie Asado"

'Twas brillig, and the slithy toves
Did gyre and gimble in the wabe:
All mimsy were the borogoves,
And the mome raths outgrabe.
    Lewis Carroll, "Jabberwocky"

Unfold the vowel towel and floom it out and let it settle on the sand. Flume, broom, room, spume, gloom, doom.
Nicholson Baker, *The Anthologist*

Practice
A. Using Gertrude Stein's piece as a model, write a nonsensical page to be read out loud. Focus on rhythm over meaning and use all the prose tools that reinforce this—repetition, alliteration, onomatopoeia (hiss, clunk, splat, etc.), made-up words, and whatever else seems natural.

B. Write a paragraph of comprehensible narrative while focusing on rhythm. Use its tools—repetition, alliteration, onomatopoeia, dialect—but refrain from rhyming or repetitive meter.

C. Read aloud a piece that you're working on. Stop as you go, revising anything that sounds off until it flows more smoothly.

See Additional Exercises: X18, X20, X21, X27, X32

The descriptive force of the right verb is enormous; it bears a kind of muscular concreteness, making the written world seem dynamically present.

MARK DOTY

EVOCATIVE VERBS

Verbs are the beating hearts of sentences. They convey action, sensation, movement. They project attitude and manner. They surprise and delight and horrify.

Be skeptical of adverbs and adjectives because they dilute verbs. A strong verb is better than a modified mediocre verb, thus:

She jumped quickly onto the merry-go-round. -OR-
She leapt onto the merry-go-round

He spoke in a growling voice. -OR-
He growled.

Example
He watched a young coyote descend from the heavy cover of timber and diagonal down the open hillside above the creek and disappear into the willows.
  James Galvin, *The Meadow*

Up past a clearing, he stumbled between two crabapple trees. A flurry of gnats swarmed his wound. The raw calls of crows—*CAW, CAW*—accused him.
  Cate McGowan, "Arm, Clean Off"

Practice
A. This prompt comes from Goldberg's *Writing Down the Bones*. Fold a sheet of paper lengthwise. On the left side, list any ten nouns you can think of.
    chihuahua
    maple
    flip-flops, etc.
On the right side, think of an occupation—like "butcher"—and list fifteen verbs associated with that profession.

BUTCHER:
cut
slice
whack, etc.

Now open the page and try matching the nouns and verbs in interesting ways within sentences (e.g., flip-flops whack the pavement; the chihuahua cuts the air with its wheezy bark.)

See Additional Exercises: X27, X31; Project C

*You don't see something until you have the right metaphor to let
you perceive it.*

ROBERT STETSON SHAW

COMPARISON

Jonathan Swift, in his many writings, almost never used metaphors and similes,
and some writers today are still skeptical of comparison language, disdaining it
as lacking purity. To my mind, this is like a mechanic refusing ever to use power
tools because they're not hand-cranked. Metaphor is a vital tool for convincing
readers of the accuracy and vividness of your created world.

A well-placed comparison not only engages the reader's imagination but
conveys more precisely the intended sense-image.

Examples
A file works by persuasion; it reduces the force of its assault instead of
intensifying it. In place of one strong jab, it resorts to a host of weak prods, one
after the other, which attack in an orderly fashion like an army of ants, with
more monotony than passion, but with no chance of a mistake.
    Fabio Morabito, "File & Sandpaper"

The vestibule door opens onto a June morning so fine and scrubbed Clarissa
pauses at the threshold as she would at the edge of a pool, watching the
turquoise water lapping at the tiles, the liquid nets of sun wavering in the blue
depths.
    Michael Cunningham, *The Hours*

Outside the rain is coming down like it's angry with someone. Like someone
had made fun of the rain's mother.
    Robert Lopez, "Everyone Out of the Pool"

Practice
A. Using Morabito's example above, take an object in your everyday life and,
    using comparison, draw out its essence. Extend the comparison, magnifying
    different aspects of the object. If the comparison doesn't work, modify it.

B. Using Cunningham's model and incorporating a comparison that acts as a
    controlling image, capture the state of mind of a person looking outside first
    thing in the morning.

C. Think of a landscape in something you're working on. Write a page of
    description, using comparisons—similes and metaphors—to evoke different
    aspects of the landscape.

See Additional Exercises: X5, X28, X30, X35; Projects A, O

If the writer depicts the precise physical sensations experienced by the character, a particular emotion may be triggered by the reader's own sense of memory.

JANET BURROWAY AND ELIZABETH STUCKEY-FRENCH

EMOTION AS SENSATION: BODILY REACTION

Which sentence is more powerful? 1) He was afraid. -OR- 2) His heart turned to ash in his chest.

Flannery O'Connor says that a writer can't evoke "emotion with emotion, or thought with thought. He has to provide all these things with a body." Finding fresh ways to trigger a visceral sensation within the reader is the writer's job. As always, the more concrete the sensory details, the better.

Examples
Shock: The pouch contained a summary of the trial, the medical examiner's report, and a separate inner pouch wrapped in twine and shaped like photographs. I opened the pouch; there was Blake dead and on the slab, photographed from several angles. The floor gave way, and I fell down and down for miles.
    Brent Staples, "The Coroner's Photographs"

Confusion: His nerve-cells pricked, his hand ached, his head was full of a crawling black fog. He felt his life as a brief struggle, a scurrying along dark passages with no issue into the light.
    A.S. Byatt, "Morpho Eugenia"

Grief: But no turbulent emotion passed through me as he spoke, only a diluted version of the nauseating sensation that had taken hold that day in Bombay that I learned my mother was dying, a sensation that had dropped anchor in me and never fully left.
    Jhumpa Lahiri, "Year's End"

Practice
A. Finish the sentence "_____ feels like…" for each emotion, trying to capture the associated bodily sensation: boredom, nervousness, excitement, panic, attraction, love, fear, betrayal, helplessness, triumph.

B. Make a list of five emotions that you've felt in the past week. Circle one and draft the story of what caused it, focusing on its precise physical sensations. Try to capture, too, how the emotion shifted and changed as some time passed.

See Additional Exercises: X22, X25, X29, X35

The chief duty of a narrative sentence is to lead to the next sentence.

URSULA K. LEGUIN

FOCUSING ON THE SENTENCE

The sentence has an infinity of forms, but each prose sentence is constrained by what comes before and what will come after—in a word, context. For example, it's been said that the point of writing a long sentence is to write a short one.

If you're not already, become a collector of beautiful sentences. Copy them into your journal and imitate their structures.

Examples
In the morning's fine drizzle, after Mrs. Fexler has led the children in their coats and scarves into the brush and back again, after they have given up again on the fire and gone without coffee, straightening their clothes as best they can and combing their hair, they all climb back in the two cars and drive out of the willow grove to the ferry.
    Mary Clearman Blew, *All But the Waltz*

It was morning and had been morning for some time and he heard the plane. It showed very tiny and then made a wide circle and the boys ran out and lit the fires, using kerosene, and piled on grass so there were two big smudges at each end of the level place and the morning breeze blew them toward the camp and the plane circled twice more, low this time, and then glided down and levelled off and landed smoothly and, coming walking toward him, was old Compton in slacks, a tweed jacket and a brown felt hat.
    Ernest Hemingway, "The Snows of Kilimanjaro"

She does not even know if she loves him. She loves his sobriety. His refusal to sing just because he knows the tune. She loves his pride. His blackness and his gray car.
    Alice Walker, "Roselily"

Practice
A. Using Walker's example above, write a paragraph made up of short sentences, each of which should be no longer than ten words. Use some incomplete sentences.

B. Write a half-page that is all one sentence.

C. Write a sentence that covers a vast amount of time—years, decades, or even centuries or more.

See Additional Exercises: X18, X20, X27

Do the best one can. Do it over again. Then still improve, even if ever so slightly, those retouches.

MARGARET YOURCENAR

REVISING

Good revising requires obsession and a belief that the work can always be improved. Before public readings of his poetry, Robert Lowell is said to have made changes in pencil to his published poems. Considering your work to be somehow sacred because it's "finished" is anathema to an ever-changing self. Allow your momentary whims to lead the way, then save your deleted passages in a "Fragments" file in case you wish to reinstate them.

In general, there are two types of revision: global and local. Global changes tend to be structural—while rereading, you may glimpse a new possibility that requires major changes and, in fact, results in an entirely different piece than you set out to write. If the new vision is, on whole, greater than the initial vision, the impulse must be followed.

Local changes, on the other hand, are incremental and recursive, a gradual accrual of clarity and power by trimming, tightening, and replacing. This happens at the level of the word and the sentence.

Some Thoughts
The difference between the almost-right word and the right word is really a large matter—it's the difference between the lightning bug and the lightning.
    Mark Twain

The more you leave out, the more you highlight what you leave in.
    Henry Green

See revision as "envisioning again."
    Natalie Goldberg

Practice
A. Check one of your in-progress pieces for wordiness. Especially challenge verbs, adverbs, and adjectives. Is each necessary? Eliminate passive voice and *to be* verbs. In addition to trimming fat, find more muscular forms.

B. Revise a piece by focusing on "suitcase" words—words that appear to hold a lot of meaning but are really too abstract. For example, "Nelson avoided personal subjects" is less revelatory than "Nelson avoided any discussion of religion or sex."

See additional exercises: X10, X15, X18, X19, X20, X26, X27, X31, X37

PART III

LONGER PROJECTS

PROJECT A – DEPICT A DIGITAL ENVIRONMENT
(Nonfiction or Fiction)

Practice imagery by vividly depicting a digital world. This can be from memory or imagination. Or you may want to play a video game or check out Second Life or seek out an immersive virtual experience to then describe. Don't try to storyize the experience; focus instead on vivid imagery of the virtual world.

For example, in his description of the video game "Uncharted 2," in the essay "Painkiller Deathstreak," Nicholson Baker writes, "It's a visual glory hallelujah of a game. Zebra shadows on leaves and rocks never looked better, nor did sunlit onion domes, nor bombed-out laundromats with puddles in them—and the shirts of the guards glimmering in the plum-purple half-light of the Istanbul Palace Museum are a sight to behold." Baker applies the techniques of concrete detail and vivid imagery to depict a virtual world—the same techniques he would use to describe the real-time world.

Similarly, in the fictional description of the OASIS, a virtual universe in Ernest Cline's novel *Ready Player One*, we read, from the main character Wade's perspective, "I finally reached the edge of the forest and ran inside. It was filled with thousands of perfectly rendered maples, oaks, spruces, and tamaracks. The trees looked as though they had been generated and placed using standard OASIS landscape templates, but the detail put into them was stunning. I stopped to examine one of the trees closely and saw ants crawling along the intricate ridges of its bark."

In both examples, references to the artificial nature of the digital environment help the reader to picture the images more precisely. Experiment with your descriptions of the digital environment that you choose. Are they better when they mimic descriptions of the real-time world and try to escape their artificiality; or is it more effective to couch them in their frame as a construct?

PROJECT B – MICRO PROSE
(Nonfiction or Fiction)

Write a new flash essay or flash story that's no longer than 500 words. Think about narrative arc. Think about economy. Think about less being more.

Nonfiction models include micro essays in anthologies like Judith Kitchen and Mary Paumier Jones's *In Short,* the website for *Brevity*, or a number of other outlets. Flash fiction models can be found in Jerome Stern's *Micro Fiction*, the *Flash Fiction International* anthology, Lydia Davis's work, or several other journals and anthologies.

The subject is completely open, the only requirement being that the piece reads like a unified whole and contains some form of conflict-crisis-resolution even if these aren't all "on the page."

PROJECT C – SQUEEZING YOUR VERBS
(Nonfiction or Fiction)

Print out a piece you're working on and underline each verb. Above each verb handwrite a list of four or five possible alternatives. E.g.:

> stormed
> burst
> crept
> slunk
> He <u>went</u> through the door.

As you review each verb list, think about the piece's themes and resonant images, then substitute better verbs where appropriate. As with any revision, you work not to highlight your thesaurus skills but to sharpen images and deepen meaning.

PROJECT D – SCENE ANALYSIS
(Nonfiction or Fiction)

Using several of the technical terms below, dissect a scene that you've written. The purpose of this assignment is to practice articulating your work in analytical terms. This helps you develop the necessary objectivity—a sort of cold reptilian eye—for judging your own work.

Length: The scene you analyze should be at least three pages (double-spaced). The analysis should be at least two pages. Thus, the minimum number of pages is five.

List of Analytical Terms for Writers

Backstory
Cliché and Stereotype
Closure
Comparison/metaphor/simile
Concrete Details
Conflict – Crisis – Resolution
Defamiliarization
Dialogue
Emotional Truth vs. Literal Truth
Epiphany
Evocative Verbs
Flashback; Flashforward
Foreshadowing vs. Telegraphing
Horizontal vs. Vertical Develop-
      ment
Imagery
I-now vs. I-then; I-narrator vs. I-
      character
Irony
Lyrical
Major/Minor Characters
Memoir
Menace
Metaphor
Modes of Characterization:
    • Direct (Character ap-
      pearance, speech, action,
      thought)
    • Indirect (authorial inter-
      pretation)
Narrative Arc
Opening (*in media res*, W's, rumi-
      native, setting)
Persona
Plot

Power Points
Psychic Distance
Reflection
Relevance
Repetition
Rhythm
Scene
Setting
Showing vs. Telling
Stream of Consciousness
Suspense
Pace
Tension
Transitions
Universality
Unreliable Narrator
Voice vs. Tone
W's grounding (who, what, where,
      when)
POINT OF VIEW:
    First Person:
      • Interior Monologue
      • Dramatic Monologue
      • Diary Narration
      • Epistolary Narration
      • Subjective Narration
      • Memoir Narration
    Second Person ("you")
    Third Person:
      • Limited omniscient
      • Omniscient
      • Objective
      • Free indirect dis-
      course

PROJECT E – CLASS PRESENTATION
(Nonfiction or Fiction)

With a partner, present an assigned piece of writing. To prepare, you should meet at least once outside of class. The presentation should:

1) introduce us to the author, including major works and any interesting info you find in interviews with them

2) highlight two or three craft techniques the author uses especially well and give examples from their work

3) lead the class in a discussion of the work at hand, especially related to craft techniques

For the class discussion, expect the rest of the class to have read the text closely and to be ready to contribute. Still, pointing out and reading aloud passages, asking questions, and calling on particular students will help get things going.

Some tips:
- Point out craft techniques the author uses that are especially useful for us as writers. These might include things like openings, power points, sense images, character appearance, surprise, setting, tension, etc. What can we learn from this writer's craft?
- For the class discussion, open-ended questions work best. E.g., "How does the opening work in relation to the rest of the piece?" works better than "Did the opening work?"
- Have a list of prepared questions, and after asking each, allow time time for the class to answer.

PROJECT F – ABECEDARIUM ESSAY
(Nonfiction)

Write an abecedarium essay that, by definition, takes as its structure the alphabet. You should have twenty-six entries, each of which begins with a different letter, covering A to Z. Dinty Moore's "Son of Mr. Green Jeans: An Essay on Fatherhood, Alphabetically Arranged" (available online) is a good model. He creates encyclopedic entries for each letter; for example, his first entry is titled "Allen, Tim," and his second entry is titled "Bees."

The essayist Cynthia Ozick writes, "No one is freer than the essayist—free to leap out in any direction, to hop from thought to thought, to begin with the finish and finish with the middle, or to eschew beginning and end and keep only a middle. The marvel is that out of this apparent causelessness, out of this scattering of idiosyncratic seeing and telling, a coherent world is made."

Seeking such coherence, use the form of an abecedarium to weave three (or more) threads together while telling a personal story. Do some research and include outside information, though be selective. In other words, don't cram in everything you find related to your threads, but creatively shape the material so that it becomes that "coherent world" that Ozick marvels at.

Some tips:

- Ground your essay in concrete details and sense images.
- Avoid clichés. Make the language fresh.
- Avoid quoting extensively from other sources, but when you do, attribute the information to the source *within your text*. In other words, don't use a Works Cited page; instead, write in such a way that the sources are clear within your essay. Better yet, use your own words.

Some possible outside subjects (feel free to go beyond these):

- Scientific subjects – black holes, calculus, insect wings, population growth
- Popular culture – TV, movies, music, social media
- Sports – a particular sport or player
- Historical event – something that intersects your family history or in which you have an interest
- "Ordinary" everyday things – pencils, water bottles, paper, computers, cars, cell phones
- Abstract concepts that you've experienced firsthand – racism, politics, religion, gender

PROJECT G – I-NOW VS. I-THEN
(Nonfiction)

The very structure of the personal essay—an older self (I-now) looking back upon a younger self (I-then)—creates the expectation that the distance between these two will reveal something significant. This can be expressed in a crude diagram where the area inside the triangle represents what has been gained by the passage of time:

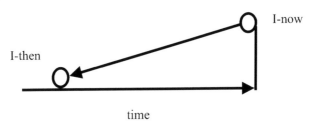

time

Personal essayists often remind the reader of this passage of time as a way of emphasizing the distance, and thus, the difference in perspective, from the younger self. In E. B. White's essay, "Afternoon of an American Boy," he couches a childhood memory within his older perspective from many years later, continually reminding the reader of this distance through phrases such as "in those days," "it never fails to amaze me in retrospect," and "Incredible as it seems to me now." The reader never forgets that this is a writer, the I-now character, casting back his gaze on a different self, the I-then character.

In this spirit, write about a childhood memory, making clear that the memory is filtered through your current self's older, reflective vantage. Structure the memory to have a narrative arc, with a clear beginning, middle, and end.

PROJECT H – LYRIC ESSAY
(Nonfiction)

In his book *The Art of Time in Memoir*, Sven Birkerts posits that the "main incentive" for lyric essayists "might be to connect with the elusive feelings and sensations of what happened so long ago." In other words, the lyrical impulse seeks meaning through the evocation of sensation more than through dramatic narrative. Chronology is less important in the lyric essay than the rendering of felt experience because it's the very rendering of that experience—the recapturing of it—that leads to meaning in this form.

Birkerts discusses lyrical work by Vladimir Nabokov, Virginia Woolf, and Annie Dillard, "past-afflicted writers" he calls them, who offer the reader "the sensuous apprehension of once-vivid circumstances and states of mind." He suggests that the act of reinhabiting past experience, including the writer's state of mind during the past event, is vital to drawing out its meaning.

With the goal of recapturing past, perhaps even elusive, sensations, write a lyric essay that restores some pieces of your past and that also seeks to find meaning and resonance between those pieces. Reawaken old sensations and mine them for patterns and meaning. Use the lyric essay as a way to restore some part of your past.

PROJECT I – FAMILY ESSAY
(Nonfiction)

Phillip Lopate says, "Without conflict, your essay will drift into static mode, repeating your initial observation in a self-satisfied way. What gives an essay dynamism is the need to work out some problem, especially a problem that is not easily resolved." When writing the family essay, finding conflict is key. Too often, family essays merely valorize their subject. While it's great to admire people in your family, frankly, it risks boring the reader.

With this in mind, write an essay that reveals something significant about someone in your family, as well as something about yourself, too. Finding the black sheep in your family can be a great place to start, but your subject might not be the troublemaker in your family; perhaps trouble has found them in some way.

Interview at least two people besides your subject. Strive to reveal what makes your subject unique, uncommon, idiosyncratic. You might reflect on or show how your subject's life has affected yours, but try to capture this influence in concrete details and in scene. Remember, don't just retell events but shape them in a way that makes for a compelling read.

Good models (available online) include Terry Tempest Williams's "The Clan of One-Breasted Women," Scott Russell Sanders's "Under the Influence," and David Sedaris's "Now We Are Five."

Some tips:

- Prepare your interview questions in advance. Be sure to ask about details that will help you evoke setting, characters, and dialogue. Contact interviewees more than once.
- Don't try to tell your subject's entire life. Narrow your focus as much as possible in both time and space.
- Precise images and insights are more powerful than general observations.

PROJECT J – LARGER-WORLD ESSAY
(Nonfiction)

Write an essay in which you explore a subject outside yourself. Create this essay in three steps:

1) First, narrow down your topic. You might return to some of your childhood fascinations or obsessions and see whether those subjects don't still feel "radioactive." Before your teen years, were you fascinated by UFOs, unicorns, or a particular TV show? What books did you repeatedly check out from the library? Finding a subject to which you feel emotionally connected is key to driving your research, drafting, and revising, and it's the energy of this connection between you and your subject that you'll ultimately try to transfer to the reader.

2) Once you've chosen a subject, do some research. Create an annotated bibliography for at least six sources. In your annotations, summarize each source in a short paragraph and comment on how you expect to use that source in your essay. This plan may change as you go, but you should convey some sense of how each source will be used.

3) Draft your essay. Be selective about the information you include from your research—in other words, don't just cram in everything you know about the subject or have discovered but creatively shape the material so that it takes on a deeper meaning. Don't forget to *show* your connection with the subject— i.e., write scenes, either from your past or present, in which you detail your connection to the subject using action and concrete details.

PROJECT K – COLLABORATIVE CHARACTER SCENE
(Fiction)

1. Create a character. Give them a name and/or a nickname.
2. Sketch the character's biography. Things to consider include:
    a. past, family
    b. significant memories
    c. items, places associated with this character
    d. deep desires, fears
    e. things you share with the character, things you don't
3. Find a partner. Share your character's biography with each other. Decide on a situation that involves your two characters and during which the two of them are at odds.
4. Individually, write a monologue in your character's voice. The character should speak openly and express why they feel so strongly.
5. Read the monologues aloud to each other, then set them aside. The monologues should give you an understanding of where each character is coming from.
6. Separately, each partner now writes a scene of the characters talking to each other. Don't forget to include setting and action. Give them something to do, somewhere to be.

PROJECT L – DIALOGUE STORY
(Fiction)

Write a story using only dialogue. There should be no dialogue tags (e.g., he said, she said) and no descriptions of action, setting, or character. Report only what the characters say. See David Foster Wallace's "Yet Another Example of the Porousness of Certain Borders (VI)" as a model.

Make the dialogue believable and significant. Each line should speak to something beyond itself, should, in effect, further the story, characterize the speaker(s), evoke setting, convey attitude, or otherwise surprise and enlarge the reader's sense of the story world.

PROJECT M – BLUE CHIP STORY
(Fiction)

Practice writing emotional realism by drafting a short story in which a single principle of "reality" is violated. Emotional realism is a narrative mode that presents recognizable human reactions within the characters.

You have one blue chip* to spend in this story, and it allows you to defy a single aspect of "reality." Spend your blue chip to break a single law of physics or accepted scientific principle. For example, in Franz Kafka's story, "The Metamorphosis," a man wakes up one morning having been transformed into an insect—not something that science would endorse as a possibility. Note that Gregor Samsa doesn't also levitate or shoot fire from his mouth: the conceit and the story would be pushed toward absurdity at that point. Beyond the initial violated principle, your story should adhere to emotional realism.

Any story that breaks a single aspect of "reality" can serve as a model, and here are some:
> Judy Budnitz, "Miracle"
> Greg Hrbek, "Sagittarius"
> Franz Kafka, "The Metamorphosis"
> Steven Millhauser, "Flying Carpets"
> Karen Russell, "Reeling for the Empire"

As the models show, the violated principle doesn't need to be a superhuman power, which is often a first impulse with this exercise. In many literary examples, in fact, the supernatural phenomenon is something visited upon the characters in a way that often upsets their lives and illuminates, somehow, the human condition.

This exercise practices building believable characters. Even if a story includes something improbable—and perhaps *especially* then—it must have compelling and believable characters. The heightened situations that result when a physical law is broken aren't easy to write convincingly, and you may have to work double-time to create realistic character reactions and authenticating details.

If you have the chance to revise the story, be alert for metaphorical possibilities that arise—cultural critiques, deeper connections—that broaden the story's meaning.

---

* N.B. The blue chip mentioned isn't real but rather an imaginary coin that purchases a single breach of "reality."

PROJECT N – STRUCTURAL IMITATION OF A SCENE
(Fiction)

Take a superlative scene from a short story or novel by a writer whose work you admire. Dissect the scene according to each paragraph's summary and function (see below), then, using your own original content, use the imitated scene's summary as a template to draft your scene.

For example, if the first paragraph in the imitation contains setting and introduces the main character, your first paragraph should do the same.

It can be helpful to use an outline like the one below to create the template. To do so, break the author's scene into numbered paragraphs and determine two aspects of each, its **summary** and its **function**, by asking two questions:

1) In analytical terms, what *is* this paragraph? (e.g., dialogue, setting, character description, etc.?). This is the **summary**.

2) What's this paragraph *doing* in terms of the larger story? More particularly, what is its effect on the reader? This is the paragraph's **function**.

Here's an example of an analysis of the first three paragraphs in Chekhov's short story "The Lady with the Dog" (available online).

Para-graph	Summary	Function
1	Introduces both main characters. Gives some setting. Appearance of character who'll become the love interest.	Orients the reader immediately to the central characters. Grounds the story in a particular place.
2	Focuses on the habits of the love interest through the eyes of the main character.	Incites the reader's intrigue in both characters. Raises the question of the main character's motivation.
3	Main character's direct thought exposes his adulterous design.	Triggers the reader's investment, even if reluctant, in the main character's desire.

Note that the analysis itself is subjective, as it should be. What you want to imitate is precisely what you as a reader find compelling about the scene. The analysis helps to pinpoint this in a way that makes its potential power accessible in craft terms. Expressing the function helps you to see how the story's mechanics operate on the mind of the reader.

Include a copy of the original scene being imitated.

PROJECT O – DEFAMILIARIZED STORY
(Fiction)

In an interview from *The Review of Contemporary Fiction*, Angela Carter says, "Have we got the capacity at all of singing new songs? It's very important that if we haven't, we might as well stop now." Carter seems to suggest that writers must continually reinvent using the tools and materials at hand, the very stuff of our culture. With this in mind, practice defamiliarization by reworking a fairy tale, myth, fable, or epic.

Consider using the point of view of the villain/monster, or some secondary or perhaps overshadowed character, and focusing on their goals and motivations. John Gardner, for example, in his novel *Grendel*, turned the epic poem *Beowulf* on its head by rewriting the story from the perspective of the monster.

Or you might cloak the old story in a new skin—that is, tell Cinderella in the vein of psychological realism by delving deep into her psyche, revealing (relishing!) in how twisted it might be. Perhaps she wants to kill her stepfamily and is only awaiting the right time when another opportunity arises…

Carter's story collection *The Bloody Chamber* contains excellent models. In particular, they give a sense of the freedom with which a writer can reinterpret and in fact reinvent stories that have at times taken on a secular sacredness.

In this, it's helpful to see the old story not as a constraint, but as a jumping-off point. Of her collection, Carter said, "My intention was not to do 'versions' or, as the American edition of the book said, horribly, 'adult' fairy tales, but to extract the latent content from the traditional stories and to use it as the beginnings of new stories."

As you draft your story, keep in mind that the point of this exercise is to use an old story to show us something new.

PART IV

ADDITIONAL EXERCISES (X1-X40)

NONFICTION (X1-X10)

X1. From Rebecca McClanahan's *Write Your Heart Out* (p.99):

> Start by listing things that are making you happy at this particular moment. Then, as memories and associations occur to you, record lists of past pleasures. Entries can be fully formed description or simply a few words or phrases: 'the earthy smell of new potatoes,' 'soft brown hairs on Mark's arms,' 'ripe pears,' 'the light that spilled from the fringed lampshade when my mother read me to sleep.'
>
> Don't be afraid to list things that others might not name as pleasures. After all, you're trying to discover what makes *you* happy, not someone else. If the tornado of dust swirling around home plate gives you joy, include it in your list. Write specifically and concretely about the extraordinarily ordinary joys that fill your day.

X2. Do a Here and Now exercise (see X16) from memory of a room you knew well as a child. Pretend, as you write, that you are back in that room.

X3. What were you obsessed with before you hit your teen years—was it world peace, ancient Egypt, the Power Rangers? Re-indulge this obsession and try to uncover *why* you were so obsessed with this particular subject. Do some exploratory writing for 15-20 minutes.

X4. Which superhero did you want to be as a child? Explore why you found this superhero's particular powers so appealing.

X5. Ask someone in your family about your birth story. Was your mother medicated or not? What time of day were you born? How long was your mother's labor? Go beyond whatever you already know. Push for specifics. Then record what you find and explore its possibilities. Is there any deeper significance for how your birth relates to your later life?

X6. Write the story of one of your scars. Do so in present tense. Then write a second section that begins, "When I look at the scar today…" Combine the two pieces into a coherent whole.

X7. What were Saturdays like at your house growing up? Was the family rushing around to go to sports events and then shopping and then out to eat? Or were the adults reading, watching TV, or working in the yard? Recreate a typical Saturday scene. If Sundays are more interesting, then recreate a typical Sunday scene.

X8. Describe a favorite family photo. Capture the physical—not only the looks on the subjects' faces but also their body language and what they're wearing. Then go beyond and project what they're thinking in that moment and how they're feeling.

X9. Practice capturing the emotional truth of a scene by recording a conversation that stands out in your memory. Don't attempt to recover the precise words that were spoken; instead, recover what it *feels like* was said. At the same time, add details in the form of beats—actions and gestures of the speakers—that feel true.

X10. Profluence can be especially difficult to achieve in the personal essay, given the reader's expectation that the presented events will be interrogated by the writer for meaning in a way that can interrupt the pure rendering of experience. With this in mind, revisit an essay you're struggling with and write a reflective note about it. What's the central question the essay is trying to ask? State it in a single sentence. Also reflect on the original motivation for writing the essay. Then ask, What's the best structure to elucidate this question? What scenes must be shown, at minimum, to bring to light the essay's central concern?

NONFICTION OR FICTION (X11-X30)

X11. Look at several openings of published work and identify the type of opening (probably one of the four listed in "Openings"). Find the most compelling and imitate its structure in an opening of your own.

X12. Write the first two pages of a new work, using, "The sky..." as your first two words. Even though you're only generating the very beginning, the opening should suggest that there's much more to come. By the end of two pages we should already be rooting for the main character or narrator in some way. And we should have a sense of setting.

X13. Draft a new piece that's constrained within a particular format. For example, Daniel Orozco's story "Officers Weep" is written within the format of a police blotter. Sherman Alexie's "Indian Education" consists of descriptions of significant experiences in each grade of school, progressing through twelve grades. Find a compelling format and use it as a template.

X14. Consider this list, from Julie Pratt, of things that engage a reader: mystery, menace, oddness, familiarity, humor, provocation. Choose one and draft an opening to a new piece.

X15. Note that where and how you begin a first draft may not end up being the best opening for the final version. Take a draft of something you're working on, identify its "type" of opening (see "Openings"), then write a new opening of a different type.

X16. **Here and Now Exercise** (borrowed and adapted from *The Writer's Portable Mentor* by Priscilla Long). Henry James advised writers to be "a person on whom nothing is lost." This exercise trains the writer in observation. The *place* in which you do the Here and Now is of supreme importance. Do it in a room, a coffee shop, outside, in front of a plant or animal or child. Here it is:

1. Write for 15 minutes without stopping. Simply describe what's in front of you, the whole scene, or one object.
2. Use all five senses but don't record anything except what you see, hear, touch, taste, or smell. Don't write opinions, feelings, or judgments. Write color and shape, sound, the feel or taste of the air, the smell of exhaust fumes. No feelings or interpretations.
3. The Here and Now connects you to the world. The more you do it, the more you refine your awareness. It's pure training in sensory observation, and it creates a concrete-detail catalog.

X17. Work on a setting description for a piece of your writing by doing research into the history of the place. Who first settled there? What's the geology, and how has the area changed over time? Contextualize your modern-day setting description by incorporating some of this history.

X18. For a current piece, create three beautiful sentences about the setting.

X19. Rework an ending to one of your pieces, using a freeze-frame description of the setting. That is, stop or slow the action of your final scene and simply take inventory of the objects or landmarks in that place. Settle the story's or essay's lens on a final, resonant object and end there.

X20. Use list sentences to enhance setting in one of your current writing projects. As you copy the paragraph into your notebook, add list sentences, expanding on the physical details of the setting.

X21. Toni Morrison ends her novel *Sula* on a sound:

"O Lord, Sula," she cried, "girl, girl, girlgirlgirl."
It was a fine cry—loud and long—but it had no bottom and it had no top, just circles and circles of sorrow.

In this vein, write an ending to a piece you're working on that relies on the close description of a sound.

X22. Find a song that strikes an emotional chord. For this prompt, resist the urge to freewrite right away. Instead, listen to the song over and over until it triggers a memory or narrative that matches the song's mood. Then, while still listening, begin to draft this new work. Fill at least two pages.

X23. Create a composite character based on two of your friends. Draw different traits from each as you describe this person physically, emotionally, psychologically. Take liberties with your creation, amplifying, intensifying, and subduing aspects as you see fit.

X24. Find an online image generator and use a random image as a prompt.

X25. Recall a powerful smell from childhood. Evoke it through description.

X26. Look at a scene from something you're working on. Take it through a global revision, questioning each paragraph. Ask: how can I make this more resonant with the overall piece? What images can I sharpen or add?

X27. Take a scene you've written and revise it. Zero in on the sound of the language, on its repetition and rhythm. Question each word, especially the verbs, and replace those that sound clunky with something better.

X28. Choose a color. Think of three things (animal, plant, or mineral) that color and ruminate on each. Then, without mentioning the common color, wend together these three in a page of writing.

X29. Choose either thirst or hunger and describe its sensation. Build a scene around a memory of when you experienced the one you chose.

X30. Find a shape in nature—a wave, a nautilus, a tree—and create a way to imitate that shape in a piece of writing.

FICTION (X31-X40)

X31. Intentionally overwrite a scene of violence. Then rewrite it from twenty years in the future. See what changes.

X32. Adopt a colloquial voice or dialect, then write a description of a setting or a character for something you're working on.

X33. Do a character sketch for an imaginary character: how do others perceive her? how does she perceive herself? how does she think others perceive her? Get to the essence of what makes this character tick. Think of this as a eulogy. Abstractions are okay.

X34. Many writers discover their short stories simply by creating characters and then following them. "I come to know my stories by writing my way into them," says Robert Boswell. "I focus on the characters without trying to attach significance to their actions. I do not look for symbols." Freewrite a character to life by following this sequence:

- Create a character. Make a list of possible names or nicknames and choose one. (You can always change it later.)
- Do a brief character sketch of:
  - A. appearance
  - B. family, including a significant memory
  - C. items found in this character's bedroom
  - D. deep desires and fears, at least one of which is secret
- What's something that the character feels strongly about? Write about this from the character's POV, trying to capture their voice.
- Read the monologue aloud.
- Write a scene in which the character's strong feelings are challenged, either by another character or by circumstance. Include setting and action and give the character something to do, somewhere to be.

X35. Choose one of the five senses and write a scene in which you practice evoking its *deprivation*. To do so, you may need to bend the rules—e.g., if you choose hearing, you'll probably need to detail those subtle noises that *can* be heard even when it's very quiet.

X36. Henry James said, "The only obligation to which in advance we may hold a novel, without incurring the accusation of being arbitrary, is that it be interesting." Consider the books that you find most provocative. Read Shirley Jackson's short story "The Lottery" or Kurt Vonnegut's "Harrison Bergeron" (both available online). Freewrite a list of the most interesting subjects for a story, from your perspective. Then choose the one you feel most compelled by, go right to its heart, and write a rough draft of the most critical scene.

X37. For a short story you're working on, write a summary flashforward ending. In other words, in your final paragraphs, cast ahead several years, summarizing events over a great amount of time and giving the impression of how things have changed in light of all that has been presented in the foregoing story.

X38. Describe a character's walk. What type of gait do they have? Is it smooth and relaxed or jerky and unsure? How do they move down a hallway or a sidewalk? What sort of shoes do they wear and what wear patterns appear on their footwear?

X39. Draft an extremely defamiliarized crowd sketch. In "The Sentence is a Lonely Place," Gary Lutz, a writer famous for his defamiliarized language, says that in a sentence "there needs to be an intimacy between the words, a togetherness that has nothing to do with grammar or syntax but instead has to do with the very shapes and sounds, the forms and contours, of the gathered words." Here's an example of a crowd sketch from Lutz's story "Divorcer:"

I had found a bench near the store and stood in quiet beside it. Others came and sat: unfinished-looking men, a pair of proudly ungabby girls I took for lovers done for now with their love, a woman graphically sad in ambitious pinpoints of jewelry. Then a man so moodless, I could see all the different grades and genres of zilch behind his eyes.

For your sketch, any type of crowd will work. Practice pushing your language to an extreme.

X40. Eavesdrop on a conversation and write it up as dialogue. Incorporate parts of it into a story you're working on, or use it to start a new story.

APPENDIX A – SCAFFOLDING MODEL FOR TEACHERS

The techniques and concepts in this handbook can be separated into introductory and intermediate groupings. Below is a suggested scaffolding model for doing so.

For the introductory course, a main concern is simply to get students writing. Early sessions should focus on inspiration, freewriting, and routine practice. After students have turned in a substantial amount of work, changing the focus to language (repetition, rhythm, verbs, metaphors, sentences) can be a natural and useful shift.

The sequences are also designed so that intermediate themes complement but don't repeat introductory ones, and a student advancing between levels will encounter only fresh content.

Introductory	Intermediate
1. Freewriting	1. Creative Reading
2. Writing Practice	2. Imitation
3. Keeping a Journal	3. Character Backstory
4. Inspiration	4. Sketching a Crowd
5. Observation	5. Reversals
6. Sense Images	6. Setting vs. Evocation
7. Levels of Concretion	7. Dialogue
8. Openings	8. Beats
9. Endings and Power Points	9. Voice
10. Character Appearance	10. Using Memory
11. Surprise	11. Writing Violence
12. Setting	12. Profluence
13. Creating Tension	13. Imagery
14. Choosing a Title	14. Rhythm
15. List Sentences	15. Evocative Verbs
16. Defamiliarization	16. Comparison
17. Repetition	17. Emotion as Sensation
18. Revising	18. Focusing on the Sentence

APPENDIX B – FOR FURTHER READING

<u>Classic And Inspirational</u>
Baxter, Charles, *The Art of Subtext; Burning Down the House*
Birkerts, Sven, *The Art of Time in Memoir*
Borges, Jorge Luis, *On Writing*
Bradbury, Ray, *Zen in the Art of Writing*
Calvino, Italo, *Six Memos for the Next Millennium*
Egri, Lajos, *The Art of Dramatic Writing*
Franklin, Jon, *Writing for Story*
Gardner, John, *The Art of Fiction; On Moral Fiction*
Goldberg, Natalie, *Long Quiet Highway; Writing Down the Bones*
Hills, Rust, *Writing in General and the Short Story in Particular*
King, Stephen, *On Writing*
Lamott, Anne, *Bird by Bird*
McClanahan, Rebecca, *Write Your Heart Out*
O'Connor, Flannery, *Mystery and Manners*
Spark, Debra, *Curious Attractions*
Ueland, Brenda, *If You Want to Write*
Welty, Eudora, *One Writer's Beginnings*

<u>Focused on Writing Practice</u>
Browne, Renni, and Dave King, *Self-Editing for Fiction Writers*
Card, Orson Scott, *Characters & Viewpoint*
Heard, Georgia, *Writing Toward Home*
Le Guin, Ursula K., *Steering the Craft*
Long, Priscilla, *The Writer's Portable Mentor*
Stern, Jerome, *Making Shapely Fiction*

<u>Textbooks And Anthologies</u>
Bailey, Tom, ed., *On Writing Short Stories*
Ballenger, Bruce, *Crafting Truth*
Bradway, Becky, and Doug Hesse, *Creating Nonfiction*
Burroway, Janet, and Elizabeth Stuckey-French, *Writing Fiction*
Charters, Ann, *The Story and Its Writer*
Forché, Carolyn, and Philip Gerard, *Writing Creative Nonfiction*
Hirt, Jen, and Erin Murphy, eds., *Creating Nonfiction*
Kitchen, Judith and Mary Paumier Jones, *In Short; In Brief*
Kramer, Mark and Wendy Call, *Telling True Stories*
Miller, Brenda, and Suzanne Paola, *Tell It Slant*
Moore, Dinty, *Crafting the Personal Essay; The Rose Metal Press Field Guide to Writing Flash Nonfiction*
Stern, Jerome, *Micro Fiction*
Thomas, James, ed., *Flash Fiction International*
Tin House, *The Writer's Notebook I* and *II*
Turchi, Peter, and Andrea Barrett, *The Story Behind the Story*

APPENDIX C – THE WORD TRAP AND THE NOVEL BY JEFF P. JONES (ORIGINALLY IN *NECESSARY FICTION*)

My debut novel, *Love Give Us One Death: Bonnie and Clyde in the Last Days,* was born out of a desire to reanimate the speech of my ancestors. Once and sometimes twice a year when I was growing up, my father would drive us the nine hundred miles from our suburban home in Denver to his boyhood home in east Texas. As we left the open flats around Dallas and entered the piney woods, the air itself changed into a damp resiny film that clung to the skin. The two-lane highway began snaking through towering hallways of trees, and everything became altered and, how to say it?—filled with newness.

They spoke differently down there, too, a speech studded with strangeness, words and short phrases — *y'all, fixin' to, here in a bit, yes m'am, no sir* — whose mellifluous sounds made of everyday exchanges things of art. Something as ordinary as a call to the dinner table — "Y'all come sit down now" — when spoken by my Aunt Leta suddenly burgeoned with personality and music. Then there were the phrases that had to be mulled over for their meaning — *don't job nobody with that stick or you'll like to get snatched baldheaded.* These strange phrasings shocked and intrigued and stayed with me for years.

In a letter that I keep in a small red wicker box, my great grandmother writes to her daughter, my grandmother Lillian, on November 28, 1920, that Mirtle "was right sick," and that, shortly after, "then the baby taken it," and "it taken all of us to give medicine" to the child. "We are aiming to move next week if it is pretty weather," she writes elsewhere, and "Miller Hughes eat dinner with us today," and "Lillian if you can spare ten or fifteen dollars I wish you would lend it to your papa to pay Judd on the mule that he let Jack have." It's a sudden immersion: the voices in this and the other family letters in the red box instantly rewind the calendar to a time when no one knows how the neighbors, with no money for warm clothes, will make it through the winter, when the family's only horse is found tangled up in barbed wire and then dies a few days later, when an uncle's gift of a mattress on my grandparents' wedding day is returned to him because otherwise he himself will have nothing on which to sleep.

Imagine my pleasure, then, sitting in the Dallas Public Library archives in 2011, holding the original notebook in which was kept, in a looping hand reminiscent of my great grandmother's, the record of a police phone-tap on the Barrow family from April, 1934, and discovering gems like these:

"Billie said we are going on a weeney roast Sat. nite"

"Mrs. B. called Nell at Barber Shop asked her what she was doing. She said Fixing my face."

"This is Mr. Leforce. Ruth said you had 2 pigs to sell. She said 'oh yes.' We have 2 little pigs we bought during the last stock show we want to sell. He said have they been around any sick hogs? She said no. He said Why do you want to sell them? She said We have no place for them when it rains."

Despite the nearly eight decades of separation, I could hear on that crackling phone line the brimming rise-and-drop in the "oh yes" that conveyed just how eager Clyde Barrow's mother was to receive the man's inquiry, and that soggy lilt in "rains" that caused the word to sag until it broke into two syllables—"ray-ens"—and broke again into raindrops making a slop of the yard.

The speech of Bonnie and Clyde's time and place was speech I knew, if not in my daily life in Denver, then somewhere deeper. Like my grandparents, age-mates of the outlaw couple, Bonnie and Clyde started their lives in rural Texas among failing cotton farms and boll weevils. Telling their story was a way, I now understand, of steeping myself in a language rich with familial connections.

At the same time, though, memory and family letters didn't hold enough word seeds to sprinkle through an entire novel. I needed a whole crop from which to draw when building scenes. In *The Writer's Portable Mentor*, Priscilla Long claims that if writers don't do lexical practice, we're "pretty much stuck with television words, newspaper words, cereal-box words." She advocates creating a personalized lexicon with this rule: "put in only the good words, the juicy words, the hot words." And for each piece of writing, Long recommends creating what she calls a word trap:

> First simply make a list of twenty-five or even a hundred words and phrases, not necessarily big words or new words, but simply vocabulary associated with that time and place and character and activity. Just making the list will help you sink deeper into the subject matter.

My word trap for the novel was a red three-ring binder into which I inserted loose pages as necessary. I divided its categories, with tabs for justice, violence, prison, weather, guns, clothing, furniture, technology, and medicine. What I did was scan relevant dictionaries, websites, word lists, books on clothing, linguistics, geography, geology, and flora and fauna, other novels from the time, the Sears, Roebuck Catalog I bought on eBay, and in these places find terms and then list these terms and sometimes riff on them right there in my notes.

Under "Cars" I find: flivver, foot feed, trigger-pin acceleration, headlamps, rear vision mirror, horsehair upholstery, twist of the key, flathead V8. A car can be turned turtle, which means flipped, or cracked up in a wreck, then junked or sold to a hockshop. Motor smoke coils. You can goose a car down the road and light a shuck out of town. With its muffler off, a car sounds like a thresher. Creek bottoms are a mess of chuckholes. The highway in sunlight is a hot slick of black. The barrow pit—the ditch on either side of the road—struck me for its resonance with Clyde's last name.

Most of these terms didn't make it into the novel's final version, but during its drafting, they were vital. I needed this word trap because it was power, a storehouse of authenticity behind the work. When it came time to pull from the word trap, of course, the terms still had to earn their keep in terms of evocation and authenticity, but I also felt the assurance that by building this personalized lexicon, no one else could replicate with precisely the same language the story that I was telling.

And on good days, doing my word work, everything hummed. Every scrap of language I came across buzzed with connective electricity, wanting to be plugged in. In 1837, Ralph Waldo Emerson told a group of budding scholars, "When the mind is braced by labor and invention, the page of whatever book we read becomes luminous with manifold allusion." Fueled by the fires of a project, the world itself lights up with meaning. We trap what portion we can.

APPENDIX D - AT THE HIGHEST POINT OF TENSION: THE ART OF THE ARTFUL PAUSE

BY JEFF P. JONES (ORIGINALLY IN *THE WRITER'S CHRONICLE*)

The writer Kim Barnes once offered a piece of wisdom that has stuck with me for more than a decade now. "At the highest point of tension in a scene," she said, "just when you've got the reader in the grip of the story, it often helps to linger a while. Take a paragraph or even a sentence and expand on the moment."[1]

Barnes's insight has blossomed over the years in my mind, touching, as it does, on so many craft elements: pacing, suspense, profluence, dialogue and beats, characterization, and verisimilitude. The idea of pausing or lingering in a scene also touches on structure—what writers like Frank O'-Connor used to call "design"[2]—and reminds me of Adam Braver's contention that "[i]t's the pieces—their arrangement and the spaces left between them—that tell a story."[3]

When and how, then, to linger once you've clinched the reader's attention? And what particular tactics have proven successful for other writers--meaning they've deepened the fictional dream and intensified the readerly experience?

First, Rhythm and Timing

The craft technique I'm interested in here is more than just a beat, that unit in a scene in which a character scratches her nose or ashes her cigarette between dialogue passages. This is something larger and different, a deliberate lingering that often occurs in a story at a very particular point—usually just before a significant action or decision comes—when the structure and movement seem to cry out for…well, let's call it an artful pause, when what fires the reader's pleasure most isn't a full-throttle drive toward climax and resolution but a move in the opposite direction toward resistance, digression, extension, delay. The ice skate on which the story rides has achieved its maximum velocity and needs simply to glide under its own momentum for a spell. It's the point during landing when, after a swift descent, the airplane suddenly levels, the thrust cuts off, and the wheels hang suspended above the runway, the pilot keeping us there, mid-air, as we feel the fullness of the tension that exists in the moment before contact.

The precise point at which to engage the artful pause is, of course, a matter of timing and rhythm, as much instinct built on reading experience and intuition as it is on experiment and logical planning. But it might be helpful to remember that the pause creates the rhythm, the break in the song helps the song to be heard. "Rhythm is what keeps the song going, the horse galloping, the story moving,"[4] writes Ursula Le Guin, and the artful pause enables us to feel, maybe even at a subconscious level, the story's rhythm.

Here, then, are some artful pauses in works by fiction writers who have invited the reader to tarry in the midst of tension. I've categorized their artful pauses into five "D" strategies that are neither comprehensive nor mutually exclusive, merely a way to anatomize their stories with respect to this technique.

Digress Outwardly

Clarice Lispector's short story "The Smallest Woman in the World" centers on an encounter in Eastern Congo between the French explorer Marcel Pretre and a seventeen and three-quarters inch, full-grown adult, pregnant pygmy woman he names "Little Flower." The first seven paragraphs describe how Pretre finds Little Flower, and they draw the reader irresistibly into the story. How does Little Flower live? How will she react to this man? What will she say? What does this strange encounter *mean*?—all questions that put the reader fully in the story's grip, and that will find answers, more or less, in the story's last ten paragraphs. But between this frame narrative, Lispector inserts an artful pause in which the story digresses outwardly, and for seventeen paragraphs (a lovely symmetry) in the story's middle, the reader discovers how a series of people have reacted to Little Flower's photograph appearing "in the colored supplement of the Sunday Papers."[5]

A woman in an apartment feels such a "perverse tenderness" toward Little Flower she could never be left alone with her, a young girl wails to her mother about how sad Little Flower looks, a boy wants to put Little Flower, like a toy, into his brother's bed while he's sleeping to give him a scare, a mother imagines Little Flower serving the family "with her big little belly!"—and there are others, each painfully comical.

Lispector's lingering digression broadens the story in a way that brilliantly and troublingly implicates the reader by suggesting that the story isn't merely about an encounter in deepest Africa—but that it's prioritizing the *reaction* to Little Flower as its highest point of interest. Her mere existence—tiny, black, silent—causes the uproar in the "civilized" world, and allows Lispector to highlight the discord between public perception—that area of snap summary and prejudice—and basic human intimacy. It's the move *away from* the current scene during this pause in which we see the indifferent and wrongheaded assumptions about Little Flower's existence that predictably infantilize her, and we're perfectly prepared, then, to have all these assumptions upended in the return to the ongoing scene when, with her laughter and joy at "not having been eaten yet" and love for Pretre, Little Flower assumes an agency that's more human than that of any other character. And it's that artful pause in the story's center—and Lispector's courage to digress and prolong at a pivotal point in time and scale—that allows for this effect.

Digress Inwardly

A digressive pause, of course, can hold closer to the scene itself and move not outwardly but inwardly. In the scene of highest tension in his short story "The Dead," James Joyce pauses at three key moments and moves *into* the deepest thoughts of his character Gabriel to track his gradual realization that his wife Gretta has long loved the young man, her first love, who died wooing her.

What the scene looks like on the page is a string of short dialogue passages and beats interspersed with short paragraphs of psychic insight. Then comes a longish paragraph that does nothing to move the action forward; it pauses the scenic momentum and delves into Gabriel's interior. Gretta says, "You are a very generous person, Gabriel," and after Gabriel touches her hair, we read:

His heart was brimming over with happiness. Just when he
was wishing for it she had come to him of her own accord.
Perhaps her thoughts had been running with his. Perhaps she
had felt the impetuous desire that was in him and then the
yielding mood had come upon her. Now that she had fallen to
him so easily he wondered why he had been so diffident.[6]

This pause for psychic access invites the reader to affiliate with Gabriel's passionate physical desire for his wife and his yearning for her to reciprocate it. "Desire is the driving force behind plot,"[7] Robert Olen Butler says, and here, Gabriel's desire reveals itself in all its tender vulnerability.

After Gretta confesses that her thoughts are on her long-dead paramour, it's another artful pause digressing into Gabriel that allows Joyce to track his protagonist's state of mind as it shifts: "A dull anger began to gather again at the back of [Gabriel's] mind and the dull fires of his lust began to glow angrily in his veins."[8] Again, no physical action, just pure psychological insight during this brief respite.

And finally, to complete the character arc of a man passing in a matter of minutes from rapturous desire to shame-filled cuckoldry, requires a third digressive paragraph. After Gabriel ironically asks, "What was he?" and she answers, "He was in the gasworks," Joyce writes:

Gabriel felt humiliated by the failure of his irony and by the
evocation of this figure from the dead, a boy in the gasworks.
While he had been full of memories of their secret life together, full of tenderness and joy and desire, she had been comparing him in her mind with another. A shameful consciousness
of his own person assailed him. He saw himself as a ludicrous
figure, acting as a pennyboy for his aunts, a nervous well-meaning sentimentalist, orating to vulgarians and idealizing
his own clownish lusts, the pitiable fatuous fellow he had
caught a glimpse of in the mirror. Instinctively he turned his
back more to the light lest she might see the shame that
burned upon his forehead.[9]

And here Joyce, with that last sentence after such a long digression, eases the reader up out of Gabriel's interior and back into physical reality and scene. The pause button has been released.

In these three longish paragraphs smoothly inserted into an otherwise action-and-dialogue scene, Joyce employs the artful pause for snapshots that capture the precise mental state of his character. Such access can thrill the reader because it specimenizes a life-changing moment from within the character's mind *as it happens*, an access brought to us in the form of psychological realism opened by Dostoevsky and others in the late 19th century. Doing so, of course, stops the action, but it's an intrusion the reader forgives as part of the suspension of disbelief that has become ingrained in the art of fiction itself.

Develop the Sensory Experience

The final two-thirds of Joyce Carol Oates's short story, "Where Are You Going, Where Have You Been?" are mostly dialogue and descriptions of Arnold Friend, the man of indeterminate age who ultimately persuades Connie, a teenager, to come out of her house and go with him—a decision that we understand is the wrong one. In this story often taught for its palpable scenic tension, it's helpful to see just how Oates employs the artful pause. She does so at key moments, two of which are included below, to heighten Connie's sensory experience. It's a way of making an already highly charged scene even more visceral and excruciating.

As we yearn for Connie to slam the door and lock it and call the police, Arnold Friend continues his smooth coaxing from behind the screen door, and we realize that at some point she will have to make a decision that will determine her fate. Then she seems to. She runs into the room, bumps a chair, and picks up the phone. It's at this point that Oates foregoes the scene's established back-and-forth of dialogue for a paragraph that zooms in on Connie's physical state:

> Something roared in her ear, a tiny roaring, and she was so sick with fear that she could do nothing but listen to it—the telephone was clammy and very heavy and her fingers groped down to the dial but were too weak to touch it. She began to scream into the phone, into the roaring. She cried out, she cried for her mother, she felt her breath start jerking back and forth in her lungs as if it were something Arnold Friend was stabbing her with again and again with no tenderness. A noisy sorrowful wailing rose all about her and she was locked inside it the way she was locked inside this house.[10]

The language is bodily and concrete—ear, sick, clammy, fingers, groped, weak, breath, jerking, lungs, stabbing, wailing. All of these words, as Oates lingers on Connie's sensorium, prick the reader's brain and invite a physical connection with her felt experience. It takes only a few lines, but as long as these are sharp and name particular body parts, the reader will likely affiliate. A short time later, we read:

> She was hollow with what had been fear but what was now just an emptiness. All that screaming had blasted it out of her. She sat, one leg cramped under her, and deep inside her brain was something like a pinpoint of light that kept going and would not let her relax. She thought, I'm not going to see my mother again. She thought, I'm not going to sleep in my bed again. Her bright green blouse was all wet.[11]

Connie's fear has become literally embodied, and it's the physical touchpoints—made clear in these few scenic pauses, artfully woven in—that help us to feel it along with her. By the end, of course, when Connie pushes the door open, she has become disembodied—"She watched herself push the door slowly open as if she were back safe somewhere in the other doorway"—and we understand that her choice to leave with Arnold Friend has caused such a strong psychic rift that she has left her old self behind and can no longer feel in the same way. Thanks to the earlier interludes where Oates broke from the established scenic flow and took the time to specify her protagonist's bodily reactions, this story packs a powerhouse ending that hits you right in the gut.

Draw out the Dialogue
In Richard Bausch's short story "The Man Who Knew Belle Starr," Mcrae picks up a hitchhiker, a young woman who calls herself Belle Starr. At a diner in New Mexico, he watches, to his surprise and horror, as she pulls a pistol on the owner and shoots him. When Belle Starr refuses to take the keys to Mcrae's car, he again begins driving her, but now the dynamic between them has shifted. Her hands remain hidden under her shawl, as we wonder whether and when she's going to shoot him—the visceral, looming confrontation that has secured the reader's attention—and the page slips into long strings of dialogue.

The hitchhiker tells Mcrae to guess how many people she's killed, and when she says "No" to his "Ten?" and waits, she prods him, and the dialogue flows on in another string:

"Come on, keep guessing."
"More than ten?"
"Maybe."
"More than ten," he said.
"Well, all right. Less than ten."
"Less than ten," he said.
"Guess," she said.
"Nine."
"No."
"Eight."
"No, not eight."
"Six?"
"Not six."
"Five?"
"Five and a half people," she said. "You almost hit it right on the button."
"Five and a half people," said Mcrae.
"Right. A kid who was hitchhiking, like me; a guy at a gas station; a dog that must've got lost—I count him as the half—another guy at a gas station; a guy that took me to a motel and made an obscene gesture to me; and the guy at the diner. That makes five and a half."[12]

Here, we've stopped seeing the characters. There are no trees or highway lines flashing past, but this isn't a pause, per se, because story-time is still advancing. Instead, Bausch has found a way to linger *within* the captured moment, of gliding inside their conversation. Because, let's admit, it's a risky move in a short story to insert a long string of short and single-word answers. To some it might come across as tedious or obvious or predictable. With limited space, each line must earn its keep, as we know, and here the lines do, but not through plot advancement. The pleasure exists in the texture of this gliding exchange. We see Mcrae's desperation in his distress-driven responses. And in her odd yet funny reactions—"You almost hit it right on the button," as well as her counting the dog as "the half"—we sense the damage she's endured that makes her all the more unpredictable and dangerous. A close reader begins to intuit that Belle Starr's not all there, which only heightens the menace of Mcrae's predicament, situated at the other end of the gun barrel as he is.

In my own writing, I'm wary of including too much dialogue. "Dialogue must always do double- or triple-duty," I tell my students. But in Bausch's story, the dialogue often doesn't develop character or setting so much as it serves to *delay* the pending action. A bomb has been set early in this drama—that pistol in Belle Starr's hand—and each line of the their back-and-forth is another tick of the countdown timer. The longer the conversation runs, the closer we draw to what we sense will be the inevitable and yet surprising end: things will not go well. In this story, nothing in the conversation between the two principal characters, despite its relative lengthiness, causes the line of tension to sag because it has been set so tight, and this is precisely what allows Bausch room to pause and to expand their verbiage.

At the end of this scene, Mcrae understands that he must continue speaking: "He was beginning to feel something of the cunning that he would need to survive, even as he knew the slightest miscalculation would mean the end of him."[13] Thus, drawing out the dialogue becomes, for the protagonist, a means of survival, and in his masterful way, Bausch has compelled the reader to urge Mcrae on in his strategy of delaying. We always lean toward the impulse to life even as we know death looms in the distance, thus the artful pause with its delaying essence is a natural ally with life itself.

Defamiliarize the Action
When Humbert Humbert confronts Quilty with the pistol he intends to use to execute him in the penultimate chapter of Vladimir Nabokov's *Lolita*, Quilty lunges and knocks the weapon under a dresser. A struggle for the gun ensues: how common this cliched moment might be, given Hollywood's heavy reliance on just such a setup. Yet here's how the first-person Humbert via Nabokov describes the fight:

> We fell to wrestling again. We rolled all over the floor, in each other's arms, like two huge helpless children. He was naked and goatish under his robe, and I felt suffocated as he rolled over me. They rolled over him. We rolled over us.
>
> In its published form, this book is being read, I assume, in the first years of 2000 A.D. (1935 plus eighty or ninety, live long, my love); and elderly readers will surely recall at this point the obligatory scene in the Westerns of their childhood. Our tussle, however, lacked the ox-stunning fisticuffs, the flying furniture. He and I were two large dummies, stuffed with dirty cotton and rags. It was a silent, soft, formless tussle on the part of two literati, one of whom was utterly disorganized by a drug while the other was handicapped by a heart condition and too much gin. When at last I had possessed myself of my precious weapon, and the scenario writer had been reinstalled in his low chair, both of us were panting as the cowman and the sheepman never do after their battle.[14]

Nabokov's is a metafictional, deconstructive move that resists our expectations—and instead of giving us two dangerous gladiators, shows us a pair of bumbling and unlikely opponents, then relishes in the literary heights of description that ensue.

Yet someone still must die, and we sink into Nabokov's playful descriptions because they are so insightfully and wittily unique. He uses language in surprising ways to make the action appear strange—the technique defined in 1925 by Viktor Shklovsky as *ostranenie*, or defamiliarization, which the online *Glossary of Literary Theory* defines as "the capacity of art to counter the deadening effect of habit and convention by investing the familiar with strangeness."[15] In other words, one way to break through cliched scene-writing is to linger on and "enstrange"[16] (another potential translation of *ostranenie*) your descriptions of the action at hand.

A few pages later, when Humbert finally gets down to the business of actually shooting Quilty, we see this technique arise again. Nabokov lingers on his descriptions. He slows down the action and describes it in a way that is purely, well, Nabokovian:

> [Quilty] shivered every time a bullet hit him as if I were tickling him, and every time I got him with those slow, clumsy, blind bullets of mine, he would say under his breath, with a phoney British accent—all the while dreadfully twitching, shivering, smirking, but withal talking in a curiously detached and even amiable manner: "Ah, that hurts, sir, enough! Ah, that hurts atrociously, my dear fellow. I pray you, desist. Ah—very painful, very painful, indeed...God! Hah! This is abominable, you should really not—" His voice trailed off as he reached the landing, but he steadily walked on despite all the lead I had lodged in his bloated body—and in distress, in dismay, I understood that far from killing him I was injecting spurts of energy into the poor fellow, as if the bullets had been capsules wherein a heady elixir danced.[17]

As with any defamiliarized image, it's the unusual descriptors and upending metaphors that engage. In these examples, the lingering occurs within the language—it's a self-referential joy that derives from being awake to nuance and connection, what Gary Lutz calls "an inter-sentence intimacy"—"the words," Lutz says, "have to lean on each other, rub elbows, rub off on each other, feel each other up."[18] Thus we get Nabokov's frisky gems "bloated body" and "in distress, in dismay" and, in the earlier excerpt, "They rolled over him" and "We rolled over us."

This type of lingering with language itself is a yielding of power, of letting go of what you intend to say in a scene in favor of allowing the language to take over and lead the scene in new directions. Such courage to release the reins can bring a new freedom to scene writing, and may incite shivers of pleasure in your process because the language is no longer being forced to drive the action forward. Suddenly there's liberty to explore, microscope in, even impede progress —all with the ultimate effect of defamiliarizing old expressions and images and helping the reader see more particularly. The artful pause used as a force for defamiliarization affords what Shklovsky called the essence of "literariness" to arise.

Lingering on the Precipice

So to return to the concept of a beat: a beat might be an artful pause, but all artful pauses are not beats. The artful pause, I contend, belongs to another species, a larger unit that steps in as referee at the story's critical points to hold apart for a moment the two opposing forces—ongoingness versus closure (one might even say opening versus ending, life versus death!, since none other than Don DeLillo has said that "all plots tend to move deathward."[19]) Just when it feels like the ending will win out, the artful pause says, "Wait a minute, there's more to see and say, more to do, more to think about."

Why should we so like to linger on the precipice? Why, when the stakes are highest, when everything hangs in the balance, do we enjoy delaying the moment? The artful pause, certainly, affords space with which to open a new angle on the story, a triangulation that can add dimensionality to the piece. Refraction, expansion, insight—all can humanize and colorize the story at its peak. But maybe it's also because the best fiction moves us emotionally, and rushing the action simply shortchanges the readerly experience. It short-circuits our connection to the characters. Like the Faustian readers we are, we crave to know the heights and depths of human experience, and once transported there, we want to feel, to the fullest extent possible, "all human weal, all human woe."[20] Pausing, lingering, delaying honors most fully that moment of suspense.

Notes

1. Kim Barnes, personal conversation with the author, April 29, 2005.
2. "Frank O'Connor, The Art of Fiction No. 19," by Anthony Whittier, in *The Paris Review*, no. 17 (1957).
3. Adam Braver, "The Experience In Between: Thoughts on Nonlinear Narrative," in *The Writer's Notebook II* (Portland: Tin House, 2012), 107.
4. Ursula K. Le Guin, *Steering the Craft* (Portland: The Eighth Mountain Press, 1998), 40.
5. This and the following four quotations are all from Clarice Lispector, "The Smallest Woman in the World," trans. Elizabeth Bishop, in *The Story and Its Writer,* Ann Charters, ed., 5th ed. (Boston: Bedford/St. Martin's, 1999; orig. pub. in *Family Ties,* 1960), 906-08.
6. James Joyce, "The Dead," in Charters, ed., *The Story and Its Writer*, 5th ed. (Boston: Bedford/St. Martin's, 1999; orig. pub. in *Dubliners*, 1914), 782-83.
7. Robert Olen Butler, *From Where You Dream: The Process of Writing Fiction* (New York: Grove, 2005), 42.
8. Joyce, "The Dead," in *The Story and Its Writer*, 783.
9. Ibid., 784.
10. Joyce Carol Oates, "Where Are You Going, Where Have You Been?" in *The Story and Its Writer* (orig. pub. in 1966), 1062-63.
11. Ibid., 1063.
12. Richard Bausch, *The Stories of Richard Bausch* (New York: HarperCollins, 2003), 168-69.
13. Ibid., 169.
14. Vladimir Nabokov, *Lolita* (New York: Berkley, 1966; orig. pub. 1955), 272.

15. Greig E. Henderson and Christopher Brown, "Defamiliarization," *Glossary of Literary Theory*, <https://www.saylor.org/site/wp-content/uploads/2011/04/Defamiliarization.pdf>

16. For an excellent discussion on the origins and translation of the term *ostranenie*, see Alexandra Berlina's introduction to her translation of Shklovsky's "Art, as Device," in *Poetics Today* 36, no. 3 (2015), 151-56. doi: 10.1215/03335372-3160709.

17. Nabokov, *Lolita,* 276.

18. Gary Lutz, "The Sentence Is a Lonely Place" in *Partial List of People to Bleach* (Portland: Future Tense, 2013), 98.

19. Don DeLillo, *White Noise* (New York: Penguin, 1985), 26.

20. Goethe, *Faust I* (Oxford: William Smith, 1841), trans. Lewis Filmore, 21, Google e-book.

NOTES

Made in the USA
Columbia, SC
29 May 2019